UNEARTHING HIDDEN MEANING

BY DEAN C. GARDNER

ISBN 978-1-965679-72-2 (Paperback)
ISBN 978-1-965679-73-9 (Ebook)

Cover painting by Aleksandre Vashakmadze.

Inquiries and Book Orders should be addressed to:

Leavitt Peak Press
17901 Pioneer Blvd Ste L #298, Artesia, California 90701
Phone #: 2092191548

A dedication to beauty, Truth, and life.

Contents

CHAPTER 1: alongside what matters

As the drums
of eternity
beckon the heart to join
pure music in the dance
of forevermore
Canis Lupis grasps
what truly matters
the way, the Truth
and the life.

As he purposes himself
into the living moment
he breathes the air filled
with hopes and dreams.

It is the power
of The Unknown God
that pyramids him
into epiphany
as the crystal
crow takes him
into life, liberty
and the pursuit
of happiness
the dynamic
of the will to be
free.

Written upon his
heart, the message
from The Spirit of Truth
opens his mind

to endless possibility.

Then, he climbs
out of himself
to ride the rhythm
of the universe
onto being toward
Truth, and twisted
rhetoric dies.

It is the doctrine
of the mindscape
to speak Truth
to power, and engage
in the liberation
of all souls.

Hearing the anthem
of hope, Canis Lupis
leaps into the war
of principalities.

Battling double
speak with the will
to be free, he fights
against the despots
who seek total control
of all and everything.

*

To gather things
in themselves
into the doctrine
of the mindscape
as the calculus

of being in time
measures the dynamic
dwelling in the will
to be, a solitary
trumpet blasts
the living moment
far into the beyond.

Then, belief in the way
the Truth and the life
emanates the purpose
to serve
The Unknown God.

Then, self awakens
to the dawn of the infinite.

To serve life
with The Spirit
of Truth, eclipses
being in nothingness
with the still life
of what matters
the artist pursuing
the connection
to beauty, Truth
and life.

Overcome by the madness
in the world
the will to be walks
with the way, the Truth
and the life by faith.

So, with no place
for twisted rhetoric

and filled with the peace
beyond understanding
the artist rides the rhythm
of the universe
to forevermore
and The Unknown God
pyramids the end
to being in nothingness.

Then, knowledge
of the mystery of life
enables the artist
to configure a portal
in a two-dimensional
actuality.

As his own always already
there mirrors within
times and a half
the always already there
belonging to eternity
he embraces the light from
a vertical column of time.

*

So, the muse carried
him into visions
onto the beyond
as she sang
the anthem of hope
and she took him
to images of self
journeying into
the unknown.

Breaking through
the barriers of time
in space, the muse
placed what matters
upon his mind
and she rubbed
his heart
with the deep touch

As the world burned
with madness, she
pointed to the way
the Truth, and the life
for comfort.

Then, the will to be
blossomed into being
toward Truth and being
in nothingness
became the no longer.

It was a celebration
of life, liberty
and the pursuit
of happiness by the world
finally ridded of double speak.

It was the freedom
expressed in pure
music that came
from the unknown
that brought the peace
beyond understanding
through belief
in the way, the Truth
and the life.

Working through times
and a half, the muse
led him through
meditation to the dance.

Although twisted
rhetoric had corrupted
thought for the while
The Spirit of Truth
brought enlightenment.

*

Feeling the abys
close in on her
filled with dread
as her spirit
dies, she longs
for deliverance.

How despair overshadows
the living moment.

How demons
haunt her, taunt her
until desperation
cripples her mind.

It is the void
in her heart
that confounds
her, although
she fights against it.

As she struggles
for survival

the will to be
surges into action
seeing the light
of a one-dimensional
actuality on the horizon
but the no longer
pulls her into
an unmarked grave.

How sweet death.

Isolated, alone
she stumbles
in silence, as she
bleeds meaninglessness
as a way of life.

Although her will
to be is eclipsed
by being in nothingness
pure music eases
into her heart and her
pain subsides.

Although her wounds
are deep, The Spirit
of Truth heals her affliction
and she awakens
to her purpose, to serve
The Unknown God.

Although the demons
bringing despair try
to break her will
to be, she prays
that she completes

her mission.

So, she heeds the call to carry on.

*

From vertical column
of time, cosmic
consciousness shines
bringing enlightenment
from the way, the Truth
and the life, as times
and a half slip into eternity.

It is with ease
that the will to be
listens to the pure
music that matters.

Pyramiding through
enlightenment, mind
obfuscates twisted
rhetoric, as being
in time capsizes
doublespeak.

Then, the despots tremble.

Then, the kiss
of beauty, Truth
and love surrounds
the ills of a nation.

As the tongue
of twisted rhetoric
burns in infamy

Lady Liberty
raises hope.

To listen to The Spirit
of Truth, liberates
the mind
from the madness
in the world.

Awakening to the glory
of The Unknown God
Lady Liberty rides
the rhythm of
the universe to epiphany.

Then, actuality fulfills
dreams with Truth
exercising the mind
with The Word.

How hope registers
in the heart
as Lady Liberty
eliminates doublespeak
and the language
becomes trustworthy.

So, she restores life
liberty, and the pursuit
of happiness.

Then, the will to be
pyramids freedom
across the world.

*

She gave the dawn
to the day
as her first light
rippled silver
in the sky
and the old man
spread his wings
to forevermore
wiping out the dread
of old age.

Although clouds
of twisted rhetoric
shadowed times
and a half, this day
cleared mind
of doublespeak.

Although at one
time dread filled
the living moment
the old man felt
pure music take
his heart to the peace
beyond understanding
as she opened the door
to the way, the Truth
and the life.

Then, life began anew
refreshed by hope.

Through her love
he learned the true
love of The Unknown
God, as he meditated

on The Spirit of Truth.

How visions
bent his will
to be to praise
the glory of God
Almighty, as he
found the light
of one-dimensional
actuality.

There was a cloudless
mind, uncluttered
by twisted rhetoric.

There was hope
written upon his heart.

Then, Olivia
from oblivion
caressed his mind
with her deep
touch.

So, the wings
of eternity carried him
onto the everlasting.

*

Looking into the center
of the crystal crow
where things in themselves
appear as the close
at hand, when times
and a half explode

into epiphany, the artist
configures the geometry
of being in time.

Celebrating the living
moment, where will
to be actualizes itself
into being toward Truth
when being in time
becomes the doctrine
of the mindscape
the artist meditates
on beauty, Truth
and love, elements
from the beyond.

Then, what matters
unties the tongue
with pure music.

Then, the voice
of freedom encompasses
the dance of thought.

Although clouds
fog perceptions
the crystal crow
emanates clarity
of Truth.

Leaping into endless
possibility by the deep
touch, the artist paints
joy and wonder
with images that dance
into actuality.

It is that being
in time was created
by The Unknown
God as the foundation
of what is there.

As linear time
in space limits mind
meditation on
The Spirit of Truth
rockets thought
into the enlightenment
found in one-dimensional
actuality, and trumpets
explode the moment
with the vertical
of time.

So, the artist
penetrates the beyond
that colors the substance
of being in time
energized by the always
already there.

CHAPTER 2: to end nothingness

As the madness
in the world leads
to world war three
and the madness
of the land of the free
and brave adopts twisted
ideologies, peppermint
birdie raises the flag of life
liberty, and the pursuit
of happiness to summon
patriots to action.

It is the American dream
that is being laid waste.

It is not a world
of oppressed and oppressor.

It is a world
of good and evil.

So, peppermint birdie
gathers the forces
of the children of God
to return their country
to its senses.

Freedom is not just
another word
for nothing left to lose.

Freedom is

the fundamental
right of all.

As the world prepares
for mass destruction
freedom fighters engage
in peace through strength.

Flexing their muscle
at the ballot box
they vote for Lady Liberty.

There is no place for hatred.

 So, the children of God
replace the despots
who corrupt the minds
of an entire generation.

So, peppermint birdie
disintegrates double speak
with the way
the Truth, and the life.

Crushing the head
of the snake, she
becomes the first
woman president
of The United States
of America.

*

So, the crystal crow
whispered in the wind
freedom

and the towers
of infamy crumbled.

Although the constraints
of oppression crippled
the children of God
they were not united
in action, as they suffered
through their daily lives.

Then, freedom struck
a chord in their hearts
and the crystal crow
reflected the American
dream in their lives.

It was life, liberty
and the pursuit
of happiness
that echoed
from sea
to shining sea.

Encouraged by
Canis Lupis
peppermint birdie
galvanized the will
of a nation.

Although once
it was a land
of opportunity
despots crippled
a generation
and freedom
Was buried.

It took the power
of the will to be
instilling the dynamic
of individual rights
that restored freedom
uniting a nation
through the leadership
of peppermint birdie.

Freedom was resurrected.

It was the destiny
of Lady Liberty
that spoke to the heart
of a nation
and the will
to power crumbled.

So, the people
voted for Lady Liberty
peppermint birdie
by another name.

*

Meditating his way
through the unknown
he unearthed hidden
meaning from the debris
left by despots.

As he read
the drift of things
in themselves
endless possibility led
him to the original

moment when all
and everything was born.

Beholding vertical
column of time
in one-dimensional
actuality, the old man
gathered five smooth
stones and headed
for Goliath.

Although no longer
a young man, he
had muscle enough
to serve Lady Liberty.

So, they counter
attacked twisted
rhetoric with the power
of the way, the Truth
and the life.

As the citadel
of infamy collapsed
into fetid rubble
Lady Liberty built
a kingdom that
the beauty, Truth and love
of The Unknown God.

It was the shining
star of history
brought together
by the will to be.

It was found
to sustain life
liberty
and the pursuit
of happiness.

Then, the scarlet rose
sang the anthem
of hope, and the children
of God danced in the streets.

So, the world
became lands
of milk and honey.

Then, the old man
returned to the here
and now from his trance.

*

Reading wave lengths
of the universe
taught to her by the old
man, the scarlet rose
sang beauty into the air
that embraced Eagle
Hawk, as he laid
in his hospital bed
his coma lasting days.

Annabel Lee held his
hand and touched his cheek.

The artist knelt
in silent prayer

at his side.

Olivis from oblivion
stood motionless
at the foot of his bed.

So, after a while
of deep comatose
Eagle Hawk opened
his eyes and tried
to get out of bed.

He had no clue
where he was or
what happened.

Joy filled the room.

Asking what time
it was, wanting to get
up and go to work
Eagle Hawk laid back
in bed, bewildered.

There was sunlight
on his shoulder.

He was fortunate to be alive.

After rehabilitation
he was ready to go on
with his life.

Fortunately, there was
no permanent damage
and his recovery

was complete.

Although his body
needed to regain strength
after laying in bed so long, his
mind was sharp and clear.

How blessed he was
to get on with his life.

*

Astro-projecting himself
far from the here
and now, the old man
eclipsed the far beyond
as he emerged
into celestial dynasties

Along side him
Olivia from oblivion
steered him toward
one dimensional actuality
as he entered times
before the big bang.

There was thunder
in his muscles, as he
flexed with the passion
of being toward Truth.

Intertwined with his
will to be, Olivia
from oblivion showed
him rivers of dream
leading to the source

of what matters.

Their mind dashed
into the unknown
guided by The Spirit
of Truth.

As they experienced
the actual
behind the real.

Although their minds
were so cluttered
with hidden meaning
only the vision
through their inner eye
could reveal the source
of beauty, Truth, and love.

So, the immediate
within a parabola
of time allowed them
to apprehend
the actualization
of their faith.

Then, they perceived
the actuality of a house
of many mansions
and doors opened
to their desire for Truth.

At that moment
they heard the cries
of the children of God
so the old man and Olivia

from oblivion returned
to the here and now
to give them aid.

*

As thunder of being
toward Truth astro-projects
into the interstices
of a two dimensional
actuality, flashes
of light reveal
the mysteries of life
and the image
of the other side
that comes from the pain
of being there
equips the moment
with treasures
beyond imagination.

As thoughts cling
to hope
all of what is there
slips into a vapor.

It is the disintegration
of trust that blisters
the moment with the ache
caused by the absence of Truth.

Then, the artist forms
the idea of want
and that image
writes the mind
of cosmic consciousness

into his substance.

As the artist goes
beyond the here
and now, and as
The Spirit of Truth
fills him with visions
of eternity, he presents
the presence of beauty
Truth, and love in earth tones.

So, the sun
reveals shadows
from darkness.

Fighting against demons
of doublespeak
his mind equates
himself with being
toward Truth
as the scarlet rose
brings life through
the anthem of hope.

Approaching the gate
of a vertical column of time
the artist colors the drums
of eternity with stardust
as he feels the presence
of the way, the Truth
and the life.

Then, beauty surrounds
the living moment.

*

In the library
of the Hard Rock
Café, when the sky
was a heavy grey
and the air was thick
with a penetrating chill
she sat planning
the road to victory
over despot oppression.

By her side
Canus Lupis opened
the Book of Life
and he showed her
the presence of the way
the Truth, and the life
into her times and a half.

So, Lady Liberty drew
a line of blood in the sand.

When the terrorists
crossed it, all hell
would be set against it.

So, after a while
they passed the line
and Lady Liberty struck
the core of the terrorists.

It meant war.

In her war room
the old man sketched
the attack against despots.

It was the obliteration
of the heart of terrorism.

Across the land
of the free and brave
the call to service
to the war effort
reached the artist
and he bore
arms in the name
of freedom.

The scarlet rose
supported his choice
to serve, because
she knew the depth
of his passion for freedom.

So, Lady Liberty
listener to The Spirit
of Truth that led
her to serve and protect
human rights.

*

It was in a college town
in the South that she
grew up as a spokesperson
for her generation.

With a style all her own
she surfaced as a force
to be reckoned with.

Being young

and impressionable
she could not
understand why
things were the way
they were.

It was being thrown
into the madness
of the world that
she rebelled against.

Although her parents
gave her a solid
background in the Judeo
Christian ethic she
could not tolerate
the folly of the world.

Where she saw
injustice, she did not
accept it.

She spoke Truth
to power
and rejected
authority that was
founded on twisted
rhetoric.

It was not
a will to power
that she embraced
but the will to be free
was the standard
that she held
in her heart.

Although she learned
that all were equal
under the law
she saw that
that was not practiced.

In her college years
took her into rebellion
with great passion
and she stormed
the bastions of hypocrisy.

In her heart
the seed of Lady
Liberty grew
strong and vibrant.

*

So, the crystal crow
that heavenly messenger
took Olivia from oblivion
to the altar
of The Unknown God
and she felt the deep touch
of beauty, Truth, and love.

Although she was not
from this world
but of a celestial
origin, she knew
the dynamic power
of faith in the way
the Truth, and the life.

Embraced by The Spirit

of Truth she found
belief in God almighty
as trustworthy.

She learned that none
are good, no, not one
and all including those
of her origin
needed forgiveness.

So, she knelt
beneath the cross
of Christ and wept
with grief.

Although she was
more evolved
than earthlings
she saw how
the elements of her
being were connected
to human kind.

As an ancient alien
successor, she accepted
the way, the Truth
and the life
as the deliverer
from haunting
demons.

So, she became
a child of God.

Then, she taught
the old man

how to exercise
the untapped source
of astro-projection
through meditation.

So, he meditated
on The Unknown God
seeing the light
of one-dimensional
actuality, the presence
of The Unknown God
the cosmic consciousness
of all and everything.

Then, he saw his
soul dwelling
in the kingdom of God.

*

In the library
of The Hard Rock Café
they gathered to speak
freedom and civil rights
into being and time.

Peppermint birdie was
there, waving the banner
of life, liberty, and the pursuit
of happiness.

Standing at the podium
she addresses the state
of the union speaking
a message of dignity
for all, and how

freedom of the individual
is a basic human right.

It was there and then
that a terrorist bomb
exploded, collapsing
the hall and hundreds
died.

Although wounded
peppermint birdie
survived.

These were perilous times
in the land of the free
and brave.

How freedom of speech
and peaceful gatherings
were under attack.

In the ambulance
Canis Lupis rode
with her to the hospital.

She was severely injured
and unconscious.

Although it took a while
for her recovery
she remained faithful
to God and country.

She would not be silenced.

As days passed peppermint

birdie came back to health
and she felt more
and more passionate
about freedom.

It was that no one
and nothing would
hold her back.

So, from that time on
she was known
as Lady Liberty.

*

Through pure music
the anatomy to the will
to be the essence
of what matters
cosmic consciousness.

Then, time in space
dissolves in a two
dimensional actuality
and a portal
to the beyond pulls
'what is there
into the presence
of the mysteries
of life.

So, the scarlet rose
celebrates times
with an anthem
of hope from the beyond
and angels dance in the heart

of being toward Truth.

As endless possibility
drops its shroud
of hidden meaning
a garden of beauty
eases across the mind
and times and a half
free the soul from
being there.

On the battlefield
of certain death
Lady Liberty infuses
the will to be
with the power
to endure.

It is the artist
who feels the presence
of the unknown
in his own mind
as cold blood mixes
with the soil of eternity.

Although twisted rhetoric
places value on the no longer
Lady Liberty celebrates
the will to be with a kiss.

So, the artist speaks
Truth to power
and the citadel
of madness in the world
devours itself.

Although the war
of principalities bleeds
life onto death, the anthem
of hope restores life
in victory over double
speak.

*

While the artist
at the edge, where death
and destruction begin
he loaded his weapon
with colors victorious
and ready to spit fire
but hot metal hit him.

Lying in the rubble
he bled his life for freedom.

Although severely wounded
he survived, a buddy
saving his life.

Although he lost both legs
beneath the knee
the artist maintained
faithful to God and country.

While he was in
the hospital recovering
he painted war's architecture.

As he meditated his way
on The Unknown God
he portrayed the brutality

of war and images exploded
in his mind.

He became an icon
for freedom and
the meaning of sacrifice.

All the while
the scarlet rose comforted
him, although
there were times
when the artist struggled
in his new life.

Consuming anger
ripped into his heart
anger fueled by demons.

It is painting that brought
Lady Liberty
to the battlefield
as a soldier defied the odds
as the will to be free
evidenced in bold colors.

While in the hospital
he refused to accept
being a cripple
and he worked on
walking again.

Fitted with prosthetic legs
he did stand and he did walk
again, his courage steady.

That was when the old

man came into his life.

*

As mind exercises visions
through astro-projection
endless possibility
appears as a voyage
into the unknown.

Throttling beyond the here
and now, he sees images emerge
from the earth of hidden meaning.

As the sensation
of being toward Truth
enters the immediate
the feeling of wonder
displaces being
in nothingness
and time, and times
and a half saturate
the will to be with hope.

So, the old man
pyramids into what
matters as Olivia
from oblivion rests
in his warmth.

It is fathoming
unconditional love
that reaches
through the universe
of ideation
as the old man

meditates his way
into beauty, Truth
and love.

Then, Olivia
from oblivion rises
into the stars
engaging cosmic
consciousness
as her will to be
rejuvenates the old
man's substance.

As they feel
the mysteries of life
through the deep touch
trumpets fill the air
with promise.

Returning to the here
and now, they burn
transgressions
perpetrated by double
speak with their faith in
The Unknown God
with overpowering
passion.

CHAPTER 3: an opened door

It is the orchestration
of times and a =half
that breathes life
into the living moment
and the artist pyramids
into battle.

As he bends a knee
his heart pleads
for mercy, as his
mind travels to the way
the Truth, and the life.

Recalling the deep touch
of the scarlet rose
he feels his way
to what matters
and how her embrace
with passion fills him with joy.

Although his soul
thrives in a house
of many mansions
he fights for freedom.

As he enters
a parabola of time
he looks upon a photo
of his love
and he hears the drums
of eternity.

Surrounding him
in his place
are desolations
of doom, but he
astro-projects himself
to the land
of milk and honey.

His reality is not
of the here and now
but beauty, Truth
and love fixed
in his heart.

Denying the presence
presented by the war
for a moment
he leans back into a bed
of stardust.

Although he feels
the anthem of hope
mortar fire
punctuates the times.

As he rests
he journeys
into the beyond
painting time
with the colors
of duty.

*

Believing that this is
the time to go beyond

the here and now
as stardust glitters
across the inwards
of mind's inner eye
the artist turns
to the old man
asking him if he
himself exists.

He realizes that he has
a past, but all that
seems to be a dream
while the here and now
is a nightmare.

In the living moment
he is immersed
in twisted rhetoric
as the darkness
of being there rubs his
mind with want to denial.

Projecting himself into
somewhere that is
peaceful, he triggers
his will to be
into beyond the war
of principalities.

Then, the artist
cleans his weapon.

How endless possibility
brings him this close
to death, he does not
understand.

Then, he colors his mind
with hope, the hope
for the peace beyond
understanding.

Then, hell fire
blasts out
as hot lead pierces
his flesh.

As the artist bleeds
into the rubble
a buddy cares
for him.

Flown to a hospital
his wounds heal
but not really.

Walking with no legs
and only stubble
is a constant
reminder that he
is mortal.

*

Sitting back in The Hard
Rock Café, in her veritable
place, Olvia from oblivion
wondered about her
home world where she
escaped persecution
terror and apocalypse.

As she took herself

from the here and now
through astro-projection
she saw that nothing
had changed.

Thankful, she held tightly

to her connection to the old
man, and the kindness
he shared.

Initially, she traveled
through time in space
searching for a new
home, a world froth
with milk and honey
where beauty, Truth
and love dwelt.

Feeling wave lengths
of meditation an old
man emanated, she
headed in his direction.

Landing in the old man's
time in space, she saw
him sitting beneath
a white oak tree
while he meditated.

Patiently, she waited
in silence until he returned
to now points.

When he opened
his eyes he saw

her radiant beauty.

She found him truly
warm and gentle.

They did not speak
but communicated
through the nonreal,
the unreal, the irreal
the antireal, the nonreal
the surreal
and the meta-real
as well as the real
the hidden meanings
reality's horizons.

He felt her grace reach him.

The old man extended
his hand and she
kissed it.

From then on, they
were inseparable.

*

At the edge
of being
in nothingness
Eagle Hawk turned
to Annabel Lee
for comfort
and he felt
the deep touch
of her loving

kindness.

Showing him
The Spirit of Truth
she reached
into his heart
with wondrous care
and he knew
he was not alone
against the demons
battling in the war
of principalities.

It was faith
in The Unknown God
that he clung to.

Although demons
tormented him
he managed to
fulfill his duties
as loving husband.

It was that work
was something
that grounded him
in the here in now
as the immediate
kept his mind
from dwelling
in the debris
of nothingness.

Finding solace in hunting
took him into battle
where all was victory

as he squeezed the trigger
on a white-tailed deer.

The buck, to him
was not an innocent
victim, but an adversary.

Bringing sport
into his life
gave him the feeling
of mastery.

Returning from the hunt
with Annabel Lee
he felt relief
from the terror
of battle
and the sense of loss.

A ten-point buck
on the hood
of his car was
his victory over death
and destruction.

*

As the sun rose
on a new day
the scarlet rose looked
to her heart for
understanding but
her mind wearied
with despair.

With her man

in a distant land
facing hell fire, she
wept at the brink
of a troubling wind
alone.

Although she supported
her man, as he fought
for freedom, she bore
her sacrifice, trembling
with fear.

Walking through
the garden of The Hard
Rock Café, she came
upon an old man
sitting beneath
a white oak tree.

He looked peaceful
and in deep meditation
as the wind buffeted
his silver locks.

As she watched
the old man with
curiosity, he returned
to the here and now
from nonbeing
greeting her with gentle
eyes and a tender smile.

They talked about freedom
duty and absence.

The scarlet rose shed
tears, alone and fearful,
and she trembled with
fear and possible loss.

She needed to talk to someone.

The old man made her
feel comfortable.

He was like a kind father.

He gave her hope
and he gave her
strength as they
shared their hearts.

*

As a thought streams
cascade into what
matters and trumpets
set the eve of being
in nothingness, the moment
slips into a parabola
of time and all
and everything collapses.

Thrown into the obliteration
of life, the scarlet rose
empties her heart
into a despairing sea
as the drums
of eternity pronounce
the will to be into hope
for life, liberty, and

the pursuit of happiness.

There is a tension
in the air
as she sails
across times and a half.

To get through
the day seems ever
so difficult as absence
grinds her mind
into dust.

Although her heart
aches for the return
of the artist, her
true love, the old man
offers her comfort.

Although their kinship bond
soothes her mind
for the moment
as they drink from each
others souls, her will
to be suffers in silence.

Looking at the paintings
by the artist
she feels the deep
touch that their love brings
as time and times
and a half splinter her heart.

She prays to
The Unknown God
for his return.

*

As the moment shifts
into half times, the old
man pyramids through
time in space, and he
traces the mysteries
of life from the unknown.

guided by The Spirit
of Truth, he passes
through a portal
in a parabola
of time.

There is thunder
in the moment
when the other
side of being
in nothingness
offers hope.

As the sight
of existential threats
subside, his mind
expands consciousness
to witness the way,
the Truth and life
filling his substance
with meaning.

Reflecting in pools
of absence, he feels
cosmic consciousness
reach into what he is
with the deep touch.

It is the deep touch
from The Unknown God
that stirs his heart
with the energy
to climb out of his
self, as his soul dwells
in a house of many
mansions.

Then, the earth
of what matters
opens to a window
of beauty, Truth
and love.

Then he sees Olivia
from oblivion
her face of stardust.

Then, she issues pure
music into his will
to be, reaching in
abundance.

As he triggers
the dawn of forevermore
she takes form in
the actual and trumpets
of being toward Truth
signal the beginning
of true love.

*

Time and times and a half
in being in nothingness

while the here in there
eclipses what matters
how the heart longs
for the fruit of the beyond.

As the heart searches for peace
beyond understanding and soul
reaches for the way, the Truth
and the life, the will to be
uncovers hidden meaning
concealed by the madness
of the world.

It was the seed planted within
his soul that led his spirit
to the Glory of The Unknown God.

Then, he found purpose
in serving The Unknown God.

Devoting himself to his
faith and filled the Spirit
of Truth, the artist pictured
a portal to the beyond.

As the image formed
beauty, Truth, and
love, he felt an epiphany
radiate though his substance.

Orchestrating pure music
in a two-dimensional
existence, he brushed
the other side of being
in nothingness.

Then, he stepped outside
himself onto being in time.

It was life, liberty
and the pursuit
of happiness
that brought him
the authentic article
rubbing him
with the deep touch.

Riding the rhythm
of the universe
he passed over
being in nothingness
and found an epiphany
in the living moment.

As time laid upon him
with the embrace
of love his will to be
pulled him to the crystal
crow, taking him to
his muse who
patiently waited.

Although he had dwelled
in being and nothingness
for a while, his purpose
carried him after times
and a half to what matters.

*

As he embraces the unknown
with passion, the seething

of his will to be surges
into the battle against twisted
rhetoric and his meditation
rockets him into the war
of principalities.

As he looked to Lady Liberty
the will to be free filled the air
with pure music, and the drums
of eternity pounded the rhythm
of the universe into muscles
of courage.
As the sky lit with traces
of twilight, the moon shone
with kindness, a friend
in silence, the deep touch
and mind worked its way
to Truth with trusting
The Spirit of Truth.

Pushing the limits
of being in time
encompassing
the existential
threat of being
there he erased
double speak
from the here
and now.

It was thinking through
endless possibility
that the old man crafted
the doctrine of the landscape
grounding it upon the way
the Truth and the life

as the flames of the eternal
light shed understanding
across the wasteland
of twisted rhetoric.

How his passion drove
him to eternity, his love
for Olivia from oblivion
filling the living moment
with mysteries of life
as his blood flowed
into the sky.

Breaking the silence
of the dark, overcast
with shadows where
infamy raged across
times and a half
the anthem of hope
brought the light
of a vertical column
of time and Lady
Liberty birthed a
promise for deliverance.

Pulling out of meditation
the old man felt powerful
mana feed his system
with The Spirit of Truth.

Then, Olivia from oblivion
danced on the roof.

*

To want to dance, to dream

of the dance, dancing among
the bulbous clouds, towering
into the blue at dawn, how
wondrous the breath
of the freedom to dance.

Looking to the center
of things in themselves
into the substance
of what matters
to the indwelling
of The Spirit of Truth
yields trust in the way
the Truth, and the life.

As pure music restores
life, liberty, and the pursuit
of happiness to being
in time, the mind reaches
the deep touch of actuality
and heart pounds purpose
into the living moment.

Simply, life is worth living.

To play the game
of twisted rhetoric
at the expense
of human dignity
destroys the soul
corrupts the heart
splinters the mind
fogs the inner eye
blinding perception.

Then, the old man

takes hold of his destiny
and slays the demons
haunting him in his times
leaning on the understanding
of The Spirit of Truth.

Probing the unknown
searching for Truth
unearthing the remains
of hidden meaning
the old man steps
out into actuality ready
to battle against twisted
rhetoric as he departs
from meditation.

Then, the old man
finding himself in
the presence
of The Unknown
God, rejoices
with the anthem
of hope.

It is the will to be
that thirsts for beauty
Truth, and love and
they are born from
cosmic consciousness.

Although linear time is
relative, subject
to change, and governed
by the celestial clocks
the biological clock
and cosmic clock

are constant.

So, because Almighty
God first loved him
the old man loved
himself and could
love another.

For God so loved
the world, He gave
His only begotten son
onto death, that who
so ever believes in him
shall have eternal life.

*

CHAPTER 4: at the edge of life

As the sun
radiant beauty
greets the darkness
with the dawn
of hope, a song
penetrates the silence
of the night, and
the artist paints
a journey
into the unknown.

With an unburdened
heart and an enlightened
mind, he configures
the splendor of what
is there, encompassing
the here in now
with the joy and wonder
of epiphany.

It is the scarlet
rose, his muse
that breathes life
into the image
of the will to be
as shadows of doubt
recede into the no longer.

Then, times and a half
slip into a dance
of splendorous form
and the symmetry

of what matters
speaks to magnanimous
power.

Then, the muse
opens eternity
to the substance
of devotion
as the artist
configures the form
of the everlasting
through a portal
in a parabola
of time.

It is by faith
that they walk
through the elements.

Clearing his mind
from the twisted
rhetoric of being there
the artist believes his
way to beauty, Truth
and love.

As the sun climbs
into the heavens
the scarlet rose
sings the anthem
of hope and the children
of God praise
God almighty
the way, the Truth
and the life
The Spirit of Truth

The Unknown God.

*

Although twisted rhetoric
dominates the air ways
and double speak is
the language of the times
the children of God
close their ears
to the dribble, seeing
through the deception.

As the will to be
storms the bastions
where deceit lies
beauty, Truth, and love
prove victorious, bringing
enlightenment to the dark
places, and trumpets
pronounce death to despots.

As being toward Truth
rises from ashes
cast by oppression
the dread of yesterday
gives birth to the hope
in the here in now
and Lady Liberty dances
in the streets from sea
to shining sea.

So, it is the dawn
restoring being in time
as the foundation
that forms the backbone

where individual freedom
sings.

So, it is the star
spangled banner
that is the anthem
of hope.

Then, the world listens
to The Spirit of Truth
blowing in the wind.

Then beauty, Truth
and love becomes
the language of
the landscape, again.

Although twisted rhetoric
had buried what matters
in the debris of double
speak, Lady Liberty freed
those enslaved by darkness.

So, it was the freedom
of the individual
that liberated the world
the power of being
toward Truth that filled
the air ways with hope.

*

Breaking into the here
in now, marching
into a citadel
where twisted rhetoric

forms the doctrine
of the mindscape
how Lady Liberty frees
slaves to hypocrisy
and times and a half
when double speak
covers the present
with a dense fog
leaves only a bad
memory.

Calling upon cosmic
consciousness, the mind
of The Unknown God
Lady Liberty unites
a country destined
to life, liberty, and the pursuit
of happiness for a world
in chains.

How a song, the anthem
of hope, opens the door
to faith in the way
the Truth, and the life.

Then, a trumpet
announces
a renewal of faith
in the land of the free
and brave as The Spirit
of Truth fills the airways
with victory over
demons of darkness.

Then, despots are cast
into dry places where

they wither into faint
shadows of being
in nothingness.

As the season
when pure music
is persecuted, passes
into the abys
the children of God
celebrate freedom
by dancing in all
the streets of the world.

The world is not
deaf to pure music
and yearns for the peace
beyond understanding.

It was the agenda
espoused by denizens
of evil that corrupted
hearts and minds.

Cast into a pit
of no return
voices of hatred
against beauty
Truth and love
find silence
 as their destiny.

*

Tumbling in and out
of consciousness
as meditation reveals

the beginning and end
of what mends the mind
and storms of the immediate
strike lightning into thought.

Then, trumpets awaken the living
moment from death's bed.

So, the everlasting traces
the deep touch into
thought, and tongues
release hidden meaning
a revelation from the actual.

Then, the artist breaks
bread with beauty, Truth
and love.

As pure music penetrates
time in space, a myriad
of songs reaches images
although neither here
nor there evidences itself.

It is meditation
upon the way, the Truth
and the life that breathes
epiphany, as the artist
forms substance seen
only by the inner eye.

The scarlet rose
his muse, takes him
into the vastness
of the unknown
into endless possibility

showing him The Spirit
of Truth as what matters.

Then, the artist
rides into the beyond
on wings of purpose.

Then, the scarlet rose
presents him with pure
music coming from
a vertical column
of time.

How his mind
bleeds images
from what is there
issued by the doctrine
of the mindscape.

*

In a center
that point indistinguishable
from purpose
believing bonds with knowing
and a trumpet pyramids
life into forevermore
conquering twisted rhetoric.

As pure music
travels on the rhythm
of the universe
hope's wings carry
images from the crystal
crow to the artist
and ideas explode

in the mind.

From distance
the other side
where blue defines
the blue sky
mind taps into
the anthem of hope
in radiant colors
bringing the immediate.

Then, the muse alters
perception to see
beauty, Truth and love.

Then, the artist holds
Truth upon his tongue
but the world does not listen.

Steeped in madness
the world plunges further
into ignorance
and it does not know
what matters most
while thinking itself wise.

Listening to the song
sung by the wind
the artist paints the soul
launched into a vertical
column of time
as the crystal crow
perches upon his shoulder.

It is the instant of the deep touch.

Without faith there is no knowing.

To know something is
to have trust.

Trust is founded upon faith.

Pulling out of trance
the artist marries
an image from the nonreal
the suspension of time
in space, the point
indistinguishable from purpose.

*

With the mountains
and valleys basked

in the light for ages
and ages, with streams
and rivers flowing
onto the always already
there, the artist folded
colors into what matters
as his muse sang pure
music into being in time.

As the sky opened
to forevermore, as time
rushed into the living
moment, life entered
a parabola of time
where a portal carried
the artist into beauty
Truth, and love.

There was the sun
in the mind that
dawned thought
of wind, water
and fire.

As energy ebbed
his skull consumed
bones dancing
in the rain
and a catalyst
erased all living.

Although the muse
more beautiful looking
and kind held him
tightly, he stepped
into darkness.

It was the helter-skelter
from the world that
bruised his heart.

It was a time
when silence smothered
the living moment
when a harvest
of being there gathered
the souls of the living
and the dead.

So, the artist felt
he had outlived himself.

Standing on his two
feet, he took his

last stand, pronouncing
the image of eternity.

Then, he saw the way
the Truth, and the life
rise in the sky, as his
muse sang an anthem
of hope, and he bowed
before the glory
of The Unknown God.

*

In stormy shadows
he walks, dreaming
the dream fastened
to his want, until
a sudden glance
at the eternal light
of his soul homes
into his will to be.

Then, images stream
through an alphabet
grounded in hysteria
and his inner eye
searches for Truth.

There is an echo
known to mindless
minds that lead
his tongue to babble.

Although his muscles
ache from his hike
to eternity, his thoughts

make ready being
toward Truth.

It is climbing out
of self that releases
him from slavery
while swarms
of hate form
around the living
moment.

Then, the muse poses
before his raw dynasty.

Then, eons count
the steps to what
matters.

In the stormy shadows
he embraces the light
emitted by one
dimensional existence
as he trusts his belief
in The Unknown God.

Meditating his way
onto the glory of God
he sees true love
reflected from her
voice as she sings
the anthem of hope.

How only the power
wielded by The Spirit
of Truth carries them
through dark times

and the walls that hold
them back crumbles.

It is the light
of a vertical
column of time
that guides them
to beauty, Truth
and love.

*

Breaking into the here
and now, marching
into a citadel
where twisted rhetoric
forms the doctrine
of the mindscape
Lady Liberty frees
slaves of hypocrisy
and times and a half
when double speak
covers presence
with a dense fog
leaves only a bad
memory.

Calling upon cosmic
consciousness, the mind
of The Unknown God
Lady Liberty unites
a country destined
to life, liberty
and the pursuit
of happiness
for a world in chains.

How a song, the anthem
of hope, opens the door
to faith in the way
the Truth, and the life.

Then, a trumpet announces
the renewal of faith
as The Spirit of Truth
fills the air with victory
over demons of darkness.

Then, despots are cast
into dry places where
they wither into faint
shadows of being
in nothingness.

As the season
when pure music
is persecuted
and passes
into the abys
the children of God
resurrect freedom
of faith by dancing
in all the world's
streets.

The world is not
deaf to pure music
and yearns
for the peace beyond
understanding.

It was the agenda
espoused by denizens

of evil that corrupted
hearts and minds
through twisted rhetoric.

Cast into a pit
of no return
the voices of hatred
found silence
as its destiny.

*

Tumbling in and out
of consciousness
as meditation reveals
the beginning and end
the artist mends
his mind, while storms
of the immediate
strike lightening
into thought.

A trumpet awakens the living
moment from death's bed.

The everlasting traces
the deep touch
into thought, and tongues
release hidden meaning
a revelation born
from the actual.

Then, the artist
breaks bread
with the way
the Truth, and

the life.

As pure music penetrates
space in time, a myriad
of things in themselves
reaches images
born of the ethereal
and neither here nor
there evidences itself.

It is meditation
upon beauty, Truth
and love that breathes
epiphany, as the artist
forms substance
seen only through
the inner eye.

The scarlet rose
his muse, takes him
into the vastness
of endless possibility
from the unknown
showing him

The Spirit of Truth
as what matters.

Then, the artist
rises into the beyond.

Then, the scarlet rose
presents him
with pure music, coming
from a vertical column
of time.

How his mind
bleeds images
from what is
there, noted
by the doctrine
of the mindscape.

*

Pulling out of meditation
onto the platform
of the here and now
peppermint birdie moved
to action.

It was time
to take a position
on her country's
state, since chaos
had burst on
many fronts.

To restore peace
freedom and prosperity
she launched
in the political arena.

Running for office
she made her mark
with honesty, and
the abolition
of double speak.

She spoke Truth to power.

Aligning herself

to conservatives
she presented
a platform
of common sense.

It was that the country
hungered for change
and the end of hypocrisy
that plagued the nation.

She attached
corruption
on all levels
to the very top.

Carrying a message
of pure music
she wooed   the populace.

Once in office
she remained true
to the principles
of life, liberty,
and the pursuit
of happiness.

Presenting legislation
to return the country
to prosperity
she won the respect
of her colleagues
and love of a nation
looked to her
with devotion.

She was a powerhouse

of justice.

*

Chasing shadows
through the unknown
searching for the veritable
when only silence surrounds
the living moment
Canus Lupis crosses
a bridge to unearth
things in themselves
as the moon follows him
to one-dimensional
existence.

Listening to the universe's
rub upon the heart – how
what truly matters appears
in particles of stardust.

When he floats
through meditation
horizons of the will
to be gather the close
at hand from darkness.

Then a song
penetrates what
is there.

Then, his mind awakens
to stormy skies, and
thunder roars in his chest.

Then Canus Lupis

envisions the deep
touch reaching through
endless possibility
and time in space
opens his mind
to the way, the Truth
and the life.

It is nonbeing
that fills him
with an anthem
of hope.

Although motionless
he feels the wind and rain.

Concentrating upon
the crystal crow, Canus
Lupis reads hidden meaning.

When he returns to the here
and now, his biological
clock chimes, with the celestial
clock always already there
in the immediate. Chasing shadows
through the unknown
searching for the veritable
when only silence surrounds
the living moment
Canus Lupis crosses
a bridge to unearth
things in themselves
as the moon follows him
to one-dimensional
existence.

Listening to the universe's
rub upon the heart – how
what truly matters appears
in particles of stardust.

When he floats
through meditation
horizons of the will
to be gather the close
at hand from darkness.

Then a song
penetrates what
is there.

Then, his mind awakens
to stormy skies, and
thunder roars in his chest.

Then Canus Lupis
envisions the deep
touch reaching through
endless possibility
and time in space
opens his mind
to the way, the Truth
and the life.

It is nonbeing
that fills him
with an anthem
of hope.

Although motionless
he feels the wind and rain.

Concentrating upon
the crystal crow, Canus
Lupis reads hidden meaning.

When he returns to the here
and now, his biological
clock chimes, with the celestial
clock always already there
in the immediate.

*

Chasing shadows
through the unknown
searching for the veritable
when only silence surrounds
the living moment
Canus Lupis crosses
a bridge to unearth
things in themselves
as the moon follows him
to one-dimensional
existence.

Listening to the universe's
rub upon the heart – how
what truly matters appears
in particles of stardust.

When he floats
through meditation
horizons of the will
to be gather the close
at hand from darkness.

Then a song

penetrates what
is there.

Then, his mind awakens
to stormy skies, and
thunder roars in his chest.

Then Canus Lupis
envisions the deep
touch reaching through
endless possibility
and time in space
opens his mind
to the way, the Truth
and the life.

It is nonbeing
that fills him
with an anthem
of hope.

Although motionless
he feels the wind and rain.

Concentrating upon
the crystal crow, Canus
Lupis reads hidden meaning.

When he returns to the here
and now, his biological
clock chimes, with the celestial
clock always already there
in the immediate.
Chasing shadows
through the unknown
searching for the veritable

when only silence surrounds
the living moment
Canus Lupis crosses
a bridge to unearth
things in themselves
as the moon follows him
to one-dimensional
existence.

Listening to the universe's
rub upon the heart – how
what truly matters appears
in particles of stardust.

When he floats
through meditation
horizons of the will
to be gather the close
at hand from darkness.

Then a song
penetrates what
is there.

Then, his mind awakens
to stormy skies, and
thunder roars in his chest.

Then Canus Lupis
envisions the deep
touch reaching through
endless possibility
and time in space
opens his mind
to the way, the Truth
and the life.

It is nonbeing
that fills him
with an anthem
of hope.

Although motionless
he feels the wind and rain.

Concentrating upon
the crystal crow, Canus
Lupis reads hidden meaning.

When he returns to the here
and now, his biological
clock chimes, with the celestial
clock always already there
in the immediate.

*

As the rhythm
of the universe
carries pure music
into the immediate
thought bends in whispers
measuring the breath
in the living moment
weighing the burden
of being there, demolishing
being in nothingness
and the sky falls
into a pit of ashes.

Although times speak
in twisted rhetoric
covering what matters

with savage tenacity
the inner eye sees
beyond the void upon
hearing an anthem
of hope.

Then, the artist dances
into eternity, following
the way, the Truth
and the life, as
The Spirit of Truth pulls
him from despair
and the madness
of the world.

Liberated from the prison
of double speak, mind
travels through the looking
glass of the always already
there to reach the other
side of pain and suffering.

It is the weight
of the world
and its twisted rhetoric
that he faces every day.

It is the will to be
reflecting through time
in space that struggles
through being in
nothingness day
after day.

As the artist launches
through the rhythm

of the universe, he
finds his purpose
as a witness
to the glory
of The Unknown God.

Although double speak
threatens being in time
the will to be conquers
the void with being
toward Truth, a gift
from the way, the Truth
and the life.

*

As the snow
penetrates the mind
and being there
cripples thought
the will to be
reaches into life
through endless
possibility.

Forced intothe immediate
the heart searches

for what matters
finding the dwelling
of pure music.

Then, times echo
across mountains
where self tastes
the deep touch

and visions
spearhead the artist
through the white snow.

There is a calling
from the other
side of being
in nothingness
that eclipses
the immediate.

Orchestrating times
and a half
into the deep touch
of pure music
the artist colors
what matters
with stardust.

Then, the dance begins.

Then, the self
escapes from being
in nothingness.

Although linear time stops
the mind circles being
there with the anthem
of hope, while
being toward Truth
carries the artist
into endless possibility.

Then, white buries Truth.

Then, hidden meaning

dwells in the artist's
presence with
The Spirit of Truth.

*

As the sun chases
time across the day
the will to be asserts
life into shadows, and
trumpets sound
the opening
of the everlasting.

Although twisted rhetoric
defines the here and now
with darkness, the light
from vertical column of time
showers Truth upon what
matters.

Although choice between
webs of confusion
confounds the times
the will to be
follows the way
the Truth, and the life
to the source of pure music.

As the rhythm
of the universe
presents Truth
into the living moment
the old man stands
before the fortress
of double speak

with the power
of The Spirit of Truth
in his bones.

Then, beauty, Truth
and love fills
the air with being
toward Truth
and the old man
listens to the pure
music of the everlasting.

It is his will
to be that climbs
out of self
to enter the beginning
of what matters.

So, he visits
with his meditation
to hear pure music
unearth hidden meaning.

As Truth thunders
in his heart, he
negates twisted
rhetoric with the power
of one-dimensional
existence, as
The Unknown God
carries him to the peace
beyond understanding.

*

Seeing through a looking

glass where Truth designs
purpose, peppermint birdie
consumes twisted
rhetoric of the will
to power as she becomes
the image of Lady Liberty
celebrating life, liberty
and the pursuit of happiness.

As her vision focuses
upon being toward Truth
she brings about the end
of being there, and beauty
Truth, and love rises.

It is the orchestration
of being in time
onto the freedom
founded upon the way
the Truth, and the life
that propels humanity
into a harvest of souls
destined to a house
of many mansions.

So, the madness
of the world attacks
the peace beyond
understanding.

Although double speak
had been the doctrine
of the mindscape
listening to the pure
music founded upon
The Spirit of Truth

grew them into
the faithful, believing
in The Unknown God.

Although darkness
had eclipsed thought
with dread, peppermint
birdie replaced what was
there with what matters.

Then, the children
of God rejoiced
dancing across
times and singing
an anthem of hope.

There is no greater
life than living
with the way, the Truth
and the life.

Seeing what matters
from cosmic consciousness
the mind of The Unknown
God breathes life
throughout eternity.

*

Composing a song
beneath the blaze
of the sun, Olivia
from oblivion
seeks to feel her way
through the unknown
as the existential threat

of being there tries
to stop her flow.

As she rides
the rhythm
of the universe
into enlightenment
she hears Truth
carried by the wind
and her will to be
declares her faith
in The Unknown God.

There is a message
in pure music
that praises the way
the Truth, and the life
and her colors reaching
through the moment
spring the deep touch
of what matters.

Then, she gathers
from being in time
an anthem of hope.

She sees that there
are far too many clouds
that shout twisted
rhetoric, but they pass
into silence when
a movement by
The Spirit of Truth
shines onto forevermore.

Soaring into the heavens

her melody releases Truth
from prisons of despair
and she awakens her soul
to the glory of God almighty.

Then, the old man smiles.

Then his pain no longer
overpowers him.

How beauty, Truth
and love, each
a gift from the heavens
reverberates within
the bones of the old man.

When double speak
covers the sunlight
with thick, dark clouds
pure music shines on
from the sound
of the drums of eternity.

*

Through the pain
brought by being
there, a lesson is
learned regarding
what matters
and the artist issues
a message painted
from visions grounded
on an epiphany
sung by The Spirit
of Truth.

There is hope
amid chaos
that delivers
the soul to
the peace beyond
understanding
and the artist
paints that
deliverance
with the colors
of the way
the Truth and
the live
a personification
of Jesus Christ.

Then, his muse
takes him
out of his pain
to a house
of many mansions
the source
of beauty, Truth
and love.

Although at times
he suffers as he
struggles through pain
he listens to pure
music in an anthem
of hope.

When the darkness
overcomes his being
in timed, a light
shines from his faith

in The Unknown God.

When twisted rhetoric
plagues his mind
he feels his way
through thoughts
of being toward Truth.

How powerful is his faith.

It is that the will
to power trembles
before being toward
Truth, and the artist
knows beauty, Truth
and love from his teacher
the old man, who abides
with the presence
of Jesus Christ in his life.

*

How she loves him.

How he adores her.

As time explodes
the moment with tears
of joy, and space
exudes the splendor
of the deep touch
they unite with bliss
onto the everlasting.

It is the unearthing
of the always already

there that blossoms Truth
into the inner eye
and their mind basks
in the light of vertical
column of time.

Sweating in the embrace
that brings the heat
of an opening to the breath
of an epiphany from
the everlasting, that showers
a feeling quickening the pulse
they reach into each other's
form with their substance.

How sweet the deep touch.

Then, to orbit
the moon
with tantalizing
pleasure, they
create the bond
to beauty, Truth
and love.

The pounding drums
of eternity
feed their blood
with juices rare
and wonderful.

They soar through
their flesh, releasing
want and need
as their senses
heave and thrust

with abandon.

How wild the moment
when they absorb
being in time as their
quick brings life
onto forevermore.

So, it is
that their child
is conceived.

*

How the muse
tantalizes the moment
when the artist probes
endless possibility
as she spreads her wings
across a wilderness
of his passion.

Revitalizing his
will to be, she
traces beauty, Truth
and love into his
heart, and he climbs
mountains of desire
as one dimensional
existence enlightens
him to faith in
The Unknown God.

It is pure music
that she tenders
onto him, as wild

times in space
excrete the deep
touch.

Then the artist
plows through
the landscape
with colors from
the unknown

It is the breath
of the everlasting
that flourishes
upon the canvas
as time and times
and a half eclipse
being there, and being
toward Truth finds
life, liberty and
the pursuit of happiness.

While traveling through
cosmic consciousness
his faith in The Unknown
God strengthens as the way
the Truth and the life
appears in glory.

Although the existential
threat of twisted rhetoric
persists, the artist
and his muse live
by the language
of The Spirit of Truth.

So, it is with passion

that they forge
their life and faith.

*

Encompassed by pain
he struggles to his feet
as each step aches
as his will to be fades
into thoughts of death.

It is not fun to suffer.

In a night in deep
sleep that a vision
appeared to him
as an angel, radiant.

It was an encounter
in the actual
the presence
of The Spirit of Truth
comforting him.

Although immobile
he picked up his
spirits, having
experienced the deep
touch from what matters.

How chronic pain
requires strength
to overcome
because to give
into it was a weakness
that he would not allow.

Some how he managed
to get to the porch
and he bathed
in the warm sunlight
following the dance
of chickadees in the air.

In the distance
he heard the call
from the crystal crow
a companion in dire times.

As the wind swept
from the south
a phoebe addressed
the day, and a red
headed woodpecker
set the rhythm
of the universe.

The pure music
of nature and
the presence
of The Spirit
of Truth brought
him a smile
although pain
filled the immediate.

*

The shadow cast by
the crystal crow brought
memories when he was
in chains, although his
mind saw the folly

of being there.

As the light of life
grew dim, his will
to be endured.

Although greatly
oppressed, he
saw through injustice
for a free spirit
cannot be caged.

Learning how to
meditate brought
him into hope
that never dies
and his quick set
life, liberty
and the pursuit
of happiness as his
destiny.

Through meditation
he gained a vibrant
faith in the way
the Truth, and the life.

It was looking through
a portal in a two
dimensional existence
that led him out
from darkness, out
from dread, that
gave him his faith
in The Unknown God
that delivered him

to the peace beyond
understanding.

How blessed he felt
at the sound
from pure music
as he heard a guitar
gently weep.

Facing adversity
he knew
as a way of life
in the battle
against the language
of demons, against
twisted rhetoric.

He found his faith
in God almighty
as the catalyst
for living a full life.

*

As the wind gusts
and the clouds threaten
the leaves, dry and brown
racing across the lawn
the old man, at the edge
of life, meditates upon
the way, the Truth
and the life.

It all is a matter
of placing trust
that becomes

a process leading to
belief and knowing.

The old man first
trusts The Unknown
God, and that defines
the mindscape
of being in time.

Looking into the center
of the crystal crow
a spiritual creature
he hears the anthem
of hope, as his arthritic
hands hold a solitary rose
blood red, a beauty
Truth and love.

Then, he listens
to the wind through
the forest.

How the search
for Truth begins
with trust.

At first, he trusted his parents.

Then, he learned to trust
himself, and that led
him to trusting
The Unknown God
as the foundation
of being in time.

He trusted The Unknown

God because he knew
his own limitations.

So, he grew to know
the heart of his faith
as the will of The
Unknown God.

As the sun peeked
through a crack
in the clouds,
the crystal crow
summoned a living
moment, and the ache
in his bones seemed
insignificant.

Then, he sat at a table
set with cheese and wine.

*

Passing into the here
and now from the far
beyond, Olivia
from oblivion read
a message from
the crystal crow.

It is that realities
were grounded in
opinion; everyone
had their own opinion
their subjective view
but actualities were
grounded in what

truly is, separate
from opinion.

Opinion is to reality
as Truth is to actuality.

Thes, reality is subjective
while actuality is objective.

The source of reality
and opinion is in
individual perception
while the source
of actuality and Truth
is from the far beyond.

Then, Olivia from oblivion
smiled as she faced
The Spirit of Truth.

As she rode
the rhythm
of the universe
linear time and space
disappeared through
a two-dimensional
existence while beauty
Truth, and love dominated
her mindscape.

The colors of her thought
revealed hidden meaning
as they formed
the substance
of what matters.

As times had eclipsed
the here and now
she soared into
visions of the way
the Truth, and the life.

So, flesh begets
flesh, while spirit
begets spirit.

It is that the actual
taught her the substance
of being toward Truth
as the purpose of being
in time.

CHAPTER 5: mirrors of thought

It is the coming
and going of seasons
as mind pursues
the other side of time
that Eagle Hawk
thought moments
and the drums of eternity
lead the march
into the interstices
of what matters.

Living in the moment
when life, liberty
and the pursuit
of happiness is
the standard grounding
what is there, that trumps
the twisted rhetoric
of demons, both internal
and external.

So, Eagle Hawk no
longer wanders through
the ideologies of times
past, but focuses upon
freedom from double
speak.

It is Truth that he
defends, as he works
his way through
the madness

of the world.

To know the face
of freedom, as he
looks through the mirror
of the will to be
enables him to carry on
as stars and stripes
wave across the land.

At one time, he v
charged the demons
that attacked freedom;
now he stands steadfast
with determination
to be part of the home
of the free and brave.

At one time he faced
the demons that threatened
freedom; now, he trumps
demons that undermine
his will to be.

So, he follows the way
the Truth, and the life as he
steps through thoughts
of what matters.

So, he bartends
at The Hard Rock Café
where God, family
and country are prized.

*

With strong conviction
for the peace
beyond understanding
Lady Liberty spoke
Truth to power, staggering
the citadel of evil.

It was an assembly
of the children of God
that gathered to select
a candidate for Congress.

There was passion
in her voice, and vision
for a country that had
gone astray from
the founding principles
of life, liberty, and
the pursuit of happiness.

It was an awakening
of The Spirit of Truth
in those who had
grown callous to twisted
rhetoric, opening hearts
and minds to what matters.

As Lady Liberty exited
from the stage, with her
entourage, a young man
lunged out from the crowd
with a knife.

Her eldest son leaped
to her aid, blocking
the assault on his

mother.

Her eldest son was
struck with a blow
intended for her.

Canis Lupis subdued
the perpetrator while
her son lay bleeding.

Although the stabbing
was not fatal, it was
a deep wound.

In the ambulance
Lady Liberty was
at his side along
with Canis Lupis.

*

Fighting the demons
that dwell in the mind
that penetrate the heart
how Eagle Hawk struggled
and the madness
of the world compounded
this dilemma.

As the wounds
that never heal
pour life into ashes
of hopes and dreams
he looks to The Unknown
God for relief.

It is the disconnect
from hopes and dreams
that buries Eagle Hawk
for times and a half
until he finds
the presence of the way
the Truth, and the life
in his own life.

So, at his side
stood Annabel Lee
guiding him into peace
through the workings
of The Spirit of Truth.

Although seriously
wounded in his
spirit, he endured.

As long as there is
life, there are
hopes and dreams
for the pure music
of the always already
there.

Then, for a season
the demons were
gone as he bartended
in The Hard Rock Café.

Feeling a sense of family
there he learned how
to smile again.

His wife and daughter

brought him love.

Then, there was a bar
fight and he was struck
unconscious, bitterness
filling his heart.

There was no safe place.

Although his recovery was
slow, Annabel Lee prayed
at his side.

To love and be loved
to work in a community
of good souls, to have faith
in God almighty, restored
his hopes and dreams
of a good life.

*

Meditating her way
through the madness
of the world, she
reached into the beyond
as pure music empowered
her with promise.

As space in time
swept across her mind
with joy and wonder
the anatomy of her will
to be revealed
an awesome symmetry.

It was the stardust
of the everlasting
that filled her mind
with the light
of one-dimensional
existence, as she leaped
into the center of things
in themselves.

Then, she sang
beauty, Truth, and love
into the dawn of all
and everything, as her
heart tuned
into the rhythm
of the universe.

S=o, the anthem of hope v
lifted her vision
through a parabola
of time, and she felt
the grandeur of The Unknown
God with her heart.

s thoughts filled
the here and now
with vertical
column of time
she grasped the substance
of being toward Truth.

Climbing out of herself
she no longer accepted
the existential threat
of being thrown
into the world, but she

took the events
in this world as a challenge
to be faced head-on.

Then, she buried
being in nothingness.

Then, she awoke
into the love
of the way, the Truth
and the life.

*

Exuding beauty
Truth, and love, she
sang pure music into life
and one-dimensional
existence eclipsed
the here and now.

As she meditated through
song, a river of hope
flowed across her mind
and thought leaped
into endless possibility.

It was that she
became a touch-stone
to the beyond, as she
witnessed the way
the Truth, and the life
pyramid into the presence
of a vertical column of time.

As the integrity

of her soul moved
the heart of the will
to be into the rhythm
of the universe, freedom
awoke in a world
that had gone mad.

She bridged the gap
of being in nothingness.

She pulled hope
into the heart
of the desolate.

Then, the ears
of a generation
heard the love
of The Unknown God
in the language
of what matters.

Ever deeper into trance
she liberated souls
in captivity, and
The Spirit of Truth
carried minds
into epiphany.

How times and a half
revealed the mysteries
of life to those
with troubled hearts
and her voice echoed
through the corridors
of eternity.

Unearthing hidden
meaning from the debris
of political activists
the scarlet rose lit
the darkness with promise
and she sang Lady Liberty
onto fountains of cosmic
consciousness.

*

As time rushes
into the debris
left by the madness
of the world
the crystal crow speaks
of beauty, Truth
and love, the elements
born from the beyond, gifts
from The Unknown God.

So, a remnant is
preserved that follows
the way, the Truth
and the life
into the peace
beyond understanding
and this remnant
is the children
of God, who walk
their faith
through their daily lives.

Leading this remnant
with Truth to power
the crystal crow

meditates upon The Spirit
of Truth, and brings
life, liberty, and the pursuit
of happiness for all.

Although the void
of desolation reaches
across the land
of the free and brave
the children of God
build a nation of hopes
and dreams as they
reject subjective reality
and accept responsibility
for actuality.

As double speak
twists hearts and minds
with the louder voices
seeking ruination of the stars
and stripes, trumpets
of Truth conquer being
in nothingness
with the power
of God Almighty.

It is not division
that the remnant
seeks, but the unity
of humanity
with the promise
of beauty, Truth
and love.

So, the crystal crow
shares the vision

of the kingdom of God.

*

Attuned to the rhythm
of the universe, as he rode
his iron muscle down
backroads of eternity
Canis Lupis felt the flood
of always already there
and he experienced
the epiphany of freedom.

With the sun
on his back
he traveled through
space in time as his
mind expanded
into the language
of what matters.

Then, he entered
a small town
at the edge
of nowhere
and he lifted
hidden meaning
from shadows
of being
in nothingness.

It was the liberation
of his will to be
from the dungeons
of being there.

His was not
the noise
of the world
but the pure
music of what
matters.

Reading the message
carved in the here
and now, Canis Lupis
rode up to a little
dinner, ordering
steak and eggs.

His waitress had a lovely smile.

She talked about how she
wanted to see the world.

Leaving her presence
he proceeded on his
thunder onto the actuality
of being toward Truth
his thoughts exploding
with the deep touch.

As the sunset
glistened with beauty
Truth, and love
he cruised
onto the actuality
of being in time.

*

As the war

of principalities
corrupts time in space
the soul of humanity
cries out, and Lady
Liberty shoulders
the brunt of injustice.

So, there is an evil
in the world that seeks
control over the doctrine
of the landscape.

As the will to power
inflicts pain
upon humanity
being in nothingness
is determined to
cripple the life of freedom.

Although the forces
of evil are great
they are no match
for the power
of the way, the Truth
and the life.

Pounding evil
into submission is
the destiny of western
civilization.

Penetrating the darkness
pf demonic powers
the light of The Unknown
God speaks Truth
to power, and stands

for life, liberty
and the pursuit
of happiness.

It is the mission
of western civilization
to bring The Spirit
of Truth as the doctrine
of the landscape.

It is faith
in God almighty
that secures the destiny
of the world
as Lady Liberty explodes
the head of the snake.

So, the empires
of power mongers
crumble in their hate
for liberty, as Lady
Liberty lays waste
the bastions of evil.

Truth shall will out.

*

To fathom the mysteries
of life, the old man
reached into the deep touch
as the drums of eternity
readied his astro-projection.

As the physics
of things in themselves

surfaced in the vision
of what matters
the celestial clocks
moved into the quick
of a parabola of time.

So, the principalities
started from the close
at hand, as actuality
governed the here
and now.

Then, the celestial dynasties
registered Truth in the inner
eye as the celestial clocks
opened a two-dimensional
existence to a vertical
column of time.

Passing through these
principalities, the old
man exited from
time present, extending
his will to be to beyond
being and nothingness.

It was the vastness
of eternity that muscled
the domain of forevermore
onto the always already there.

To unearth hidden
meaning, the old
man pyramided
himself through
the unknown, and

onto the redemption
of time.

Time past and time future
were redeemed through
time present, as the old
man opened his heart
to the way, the Truth
and the life.

Feeling the surfacing
of the mysteries of life
he launched into
pure music as he
followed it with the
presence of The Spirit
of Truth.

Then, from the looking
glass of being toward
Truth, his inner eye
ferreted out what
matters.

*

Launched into the unknown
as he rode the rhythm
of the universe to the other
side of being in time
he came to a forest
rich in the mysteries of life.

There was a glow
to the trees
as a breeze carried

thought endowed
with stardust.

Walking through
the woodlands
of what was there
he came upon an altar
to The Unknown God
as trees spoke
beauty, Truth, and love
into the immediate.

Then, an anthem
of hope broke through
the leaves, and the scarlet
rose appeared wearing
a gown of splendor.

As the sun set
bringing the shadows
of darkness, she spoke
Truth to power
and a hard rain fell.

Rubbing his sensibility
with curiosity
he listened to the voice
of what matters
and the scarlet rose
led him to the way
the Truth, and the life.

As he entered
deep trance
he believed
himself into things

in themselves
and the authentic
article of being
toward Truth
encompassed
times and a half.

It was the feeling
of a message
written upon his
heart that pyramided
him onto forevermore.

Then, he saw all
and everything implode
into one-dimensional
existence and a vertical
column of time leading him
to the glory of God almighty.

*

As the love
of The Unknown God
surfaced as the greatest
mystery of life
Annabel Lee saw
beauty, Truth
and love, while she
meditated her way
through what was there.

Seeing the light
of one-dimensional
existence, she pulled
what matters with the will

to be into her thoughts
as her minds harvested
hopes and dreams.

It was the undeniable
actuality of the way
the Truth and the life
that took her
to the other side
of being in nothingness.

Although she felt
despair at the waywardness
of the coming generation
she grew her daughter
as a child of God.

Although Eagle Hawk
fought for freedom
in Vietnam, he listened
to current trends
of racism and antisemitism
with repulsion.

As activists stormed
the citadels of Truth
demanding for the freedom
of Palestine
he knew that all
oppression was wrong
but he also believed
that Israel had
the right to exist.

It was the corruption
of high places that

spoke double speak
to the people
of the free and brave.

Annabel Lee and Eagle
Hawk both cringed
at the direction
of some youth
who denied the rights
to live and let live.

To deny the Truth
of history, they saw
as a symptom
of ignorance.

So, who are
the authors
of history
and who
the authors
of Truth?

*

Upon the stage
of being in time
where life, liberty
and the pursuit
of happiness fade
into the darkness
of the corrupt
hidden meaning
flourishes
in the heart
of twisted rhetoric

and the will
to power buries Truth.

As the will to be
conforms to the rubric
of double speak
and the lemmings
rush into the sea
the individual is lost
in a quagmire of hate.

Always in search
for a cause, youth
leaps into popular
trends, ever so blindly
ignoring Truth.

How the hateful heart
devours Truth
until the world
drowns in blood.

It is that life
liberty, and the pursuit
of happiness is
founded as Western
Civilization when it is
time to pull the head
out of the sand
and look at hate
as the ruination
of mankind.

So, on October seventh
2023, the Truth
of freedom was raped.

Burying the being toward
Truth became the doctrine
of the landscape as live
and let live writhed in torture.

It is a war
of principalities
where the will
to power murders
what matters.

So, the blind
seek the blood
of Lady Liberty.

*

Astro-projecting herself
from the beyond
Olivia from oblivion
searched the brainwaves
for a soul of beauty
Truth, and love.

As time rolled down
from eternity through
a parabola of time
she focused
on the emissions
of the old man
where he meditated
on the peace
beyond understanding.

Powered by the physics
of always already there

she landed beside
an old man meditating
beneath a white oak tree.

Although he dwelled
in three-dimensional
existence, Olivia
from oblivion allowed
herself to experience
his life.

She saw how
his faith surpassed
the here and now.

She felt his heart
pound life
into the living moment.

She knew him
as his will to be
painted the colors
of forevermore.

Then, she entered
his presence
opening his heart
to true love.

Seeing her face
he gathered
times and a half
when the mystery
of life unearthed
hidden meaning

and he knew
her as a vision
of what matters.

Then, they became one.

*

Centering on the actual
where the experiential
of the close at hand
determines the thing
in-itself, including
the hidden meaning
of what matters
the old man carves
the mysteries of life
into the heart of being
toward Truth.

So, the determination
of whether something
is or is not of the actual
grounds itself in the inner
eye, the looking glass
of endless possibility.

It is the opposition
of the actual to
the universe
of the unreal
defined by the negation
of a positing.

To know what is
predetermines

the possibility
of not there
as the cognition
of the unreal relies
on the negation
of the experiential.

Consequentially, one
does not primordially
know what is the unreal
as endless possibility
grounds itself
in the domain
of the meta-real.

It is through the meta-real
the domain of the imaginary
that allows the probing
of the unknown.

To trust what is there
proceeds from
understanding what
matters.

It is the real
that contains
the actual
as witnessed through
the inner eye as language
explores the unknown
through the meta-real.

That which is not
of the actual does not exist
except in the imaginary.

*

As the energy
of the will to be
surges forward
and times and a half
measure the moment
in stardust
hopes and dreams
flourish in the liberty
of being toward Truth.

It is the absence
of purpose
that defines being
in nothingness
as the despair
when there are
no hopes
and no dreams.

It is tyranny
of twisted rhetoric
that bleeds dry
the veritable
in being in time
as silence
pounds death
into the living moment.

Then the language
of forevermore
speaks Truth
into the always
already there.

As space in time
throttles what matters
into the center
of things in themselves
mind thinks its way
into the nonreal, and
the aperture of the inner
eye releases visions
of forevermore.

It is an epiphany
filled with The Spirit
of Truth that writes
faith in The Unknown
God.

Although there is
treachery
in being in nothingness
the way, the Truth
and the life carries
the soul to a house
of many mansions
where the peace
beyond understanding
fills the nonreal
with the everlasting.

So, the language of beauty
Truth, and love emanates
from The Unknown God.

*

As the void
of being in

nothingness
dominates his
thoughts with
hopelessness
he felt the despair
of outliving himself.

Leaving the actual
of endless possibility
his mind dabbled
with the no longer
as the bare
bones of subsistence
shattered beneath
the weight of his reality.

It was when his mind
felt inert and not living
his life as an experiment
in the experiential
that he did not gather
the hope of another day.

As the chill
of darkness
consumed his
self, his blood
turned into ice.

Although the ache
of being there
ripped across
his form
his substance
heard the pure
music from

the beyond.

It was the anthem of hope.

Then, he saw
the face
of an angel
and she took
his heart
to a land of milk
and honey.

Although he had
lost his will
to be for a while
her smile restored
his sense of life.

To feel desire
awakened his
thoughts to
being toward
Truth.

Then, he left dread
to enter endless possibility
with a song in his heart.

*

Rooted in the center
of things in themselves
the actual registers
what matters
as the inner
eye liberates self

from the tyranny
of being there.

So, there is subjective
reality and consensus
reality and the actual
co-existing in thought
as meditation reveals
The Spirit of Truth.

It is the snare
of being there
that traps thought
in a quagmire
of confusion.

If something is
many things
the integrity
of the thing
in itself ceases
to exist; it is not.

Although there are
a number of realities
there is only one actuality.

As what matters
in actuality speaks
of beauty, Truth
and love, the living
moment enables the self
to believe itself beyond
the abys, and onto
pure music.

Then, The Spirit
of Truth eases
into the heart
as mind leaps
to new horizons.

Then, time future
redeems time
onto the everlasting
and the drums
of eternity march
into the war
of principalities.

It is the battle
of ideas that defines
the horizons of time
as the actual in the war
of principalities
determines the freedom
of being toward Truth.

CHAPTER 6: to fight the will to power

In the moment when
space in time collapses
when being in time
drifts into the abys
the will to be turns
to the way, the Truth
and the life for the peace
beyond understanding.

Struck by the power
wielded by being there
the will to be stands
in a forest of Truth
as the place that matters.

There had been only
silence to the moment.

Then, he feels
the rhythm
of the universe
carry him
into the domain
of pure music.

As thoughts no
longer were scrambled
and clarity focused
upon beauty, Truth
and love, his will
to be held onto faith
in The Unknown God.

Casting aside
all constraints
he rises armed
with a mind destined
to conquer the savage
attacks by twisted
rhetoric, although
he bleeds with pain
from battle.

So, it is the war
of principalities
that he faces.

So, it is the fight
against the will
to power that
manipulates
language, replacing
what is there
with dissonate noise.

Identifying what is
as multiple realities
until mind is
lost in the babble
of double speak
his will to be aligns
itself with the actual
leaving the virtual
while grounded in
the veritable.

*

How the mysteries

of life peak curiosity
as wonders cascade
across mind, as the wind
speaks endless possibility
into the living moment.

It is the blue of the sky
that defines what matters.

It is a lone
cloud that measures
the passing of time
and the artist listens
to the earth groan
with the essential Truth.

As the sunshine
awakens thought
to hidden meaning
the heart yearns
for the peace beyond
understanding.

As the wind
through the trees
breathes Truth
the artist listens
hungry for more.

Although there
are shadows
clinging to twisted
rhetoric, that confound
times and a half
that hide what
matters, the artist

paints the beyond
with pure music.

To hear the song
of hope penetrate
being there with passion
the will to be stands tall
among a stand of trees.

Then, the wind
carries the anthem
of hope into
the immediate
and the artist
bleeds Truth
into the passion
for freedom.

Then, the artist
hears the crystal
crow announce life
liberty, and the pursuit
of happiness for all.

*

In the moment
when pure music
opens times
to understanding
and the threshold
of the deep
touch reaches
into the will
to be with promise
self actualizes itself

into being toward
Truth, and the rhythm
of the universe
drives life into
a one-dimensional
existence.

It is the death
of being there
and the birth
of what matters.

It is the orchestration
of images into
an anthem of hope.

As the artist probes
the unknown with
colors of passion
the world witnesses
the actual in
the living moment.

How the veritable
eclipses shadows
that haunt times.

Then, the artist
designs time
with the energy
launched from
the beyond
and he forms
the substance
of the deep touch
in a two-dimensional

existence.

It is there
that a portal
carries thought
into images
of forevermore
the flourishing
of faith in
The Unknown God.

Although death ends
in silence
the way, the Truth
and the life
delivers the faithful
to the glory
of God almighty
and the presence of
pure music forevermore.

*

Feeding a wilderness
of thought with the energy
found in the actualization
of space in time
they consume darkness
with the light of Truth.

Armed with The Spirit
of Truth, they vanquish
the existential threat
of being in nothingness
and the dread that
belongs to it.

although the madness
of the world staggers
the living moment
as futility attacks
the heart, the will
to be stands tall.

Listening to pure
music trumpeting
the rhythm
of the universe
they march onto
bastions of despair
victorious with
the blood of
what matters.

It is the substance
of Truth over powers
the will to power
as life, liberty
and the pursuit
of happiness are
their legacy
for all times.

It is that freedom
restores dry bones
to life, as Truth
liberates the soul.

Then, the children
of God dance
to pure music
showering from
the heavens.

Then, time and times
and a half witness
the way, the Truth
and the life coming
from glory to
the here and now.

How blessed the thoughts
from cosmic consciousness
onto their mind as eternity
grows in their heart.

*

As the world spins
reckless with disorder
twisted rhetoric casts
darkness over the light
of being in time
and the will to be
dangles over flames
of indecision.

To see Truth bleed
in avenues of dreams
and to hear trumpets
of hope silenced
how dismal the future
without the way
the Truth, and the life.

So, minds yearn
for meaning
while hearts weep.

As rivers of doubt

pollute times
as seas writhe
with madness
as the sky cries
out in pain
how being there
corrupts what
matters.

So, the artist
paints the existential
moment with the blood
of the will to be
coloring hope with
the graves
of the destitute.

Then, his inner eye
looks into things
in themselves
and Truth echoes
in his skull.

Then, his purpose leads
him to unearth his faith.

It is his will
to be that connects
him to the other
side of being in
nothingness
as his heart fills
with The Spirit
of Truth.

Although the world

screams with depravity
the artist's purpose
is defined by service
to The Unknown God.

*

As a stand of trees
reaches into the sky
and the compass
of eternity points
to the here and now
Olivia from oblivion
astro-projects
into the beyond.

There is quiet
to the moment
as the heart
soars into what
matters.

Her inner eye
focuses upon
the peace beyond
understanding through
her faith in the way
the Truth, and the life.

Then, she looks
through celestial
principalities
with an over
powering hunger.

Then, space in time

pass by, as she
configures thought
with prayer to
The Unknown God.

Although far
into the unknown
she feel the pulse
that governs
the here and now
and the scent
of Truth purifies
her will to be.

How her hunger
for Truth grew
into a connection
with the deep touch.

It was that the heavens
smiled upon her.

It was that The Spirit
of Truth danced
in her heart.

Drifting through
pure music, she
tasted what
the mysteries
of life were
all about.

Then, she closed
her eyes for a moment
upon feeling the presence

of The Unknown God.

*

In the quiet
when the heart
stirs with the mysteries
of life, the melody
of meaning whispers
from the catacombs
of Truth.

To unearth the purpose
of her will to be
she waits for pure
music to connect
the here and now
to the beyond.

How wonder fills
time present
with the dance
of hope, as she leans
on the understanding
of the way, the Truth
and the life.

Then, listening
to the anthem
of hope, she
rises through
a parabola of time
onto the threshold
of what matters.

Then, a trumpet sounds

pronouncing being
toward Truth
as the purpose
behind being in time.

As the always
already there
appears on
the horizon
she leaves
the existential
threat of being
in nothingness
to venture
into endless
possibility.

It is through time
that she uncovers
what matters
from the debris
of being there.

How the drift
of thought
through what is
there opens her mind
to Truth, while her
inner eye secures
a look to The Spirit
of Truth.

*

It is the call
through the darkness

that the crystal
crow announces living
in the always
already there
as the will to be
rises with the dawn
of all and nothingness.

It is seeing
through the immediate
that the mind
releases being in time
despite twisted rhetoric.

Then, the old man
climbs into visions
of eternity
a life living in joy
and wonder.

Wandering through
a wilderness of thought
he opens himself
to the glory
of he Unknown God
after being called
to faith, as a trumpet
of Truth blasts the actual
into times and a half.

Looking through
the looking glass
that defines
the mysteries
of life, he unearths
the geometry

of what matters
and the rhythm
of the universe
carries him
into epiphany.

As the crystal crow
uncovers hidden
meaning, the old
man awakens
to the presence
of the way, the Truth
and the life.

Then, he sees
his purpose as being
toward Truth.

Feeling the presence
of The Spirit of Truth
in the here and now
the old man lives
a life of beauty, Truth
and love.

*

Through the looking
glass of reality, Truth
is subjective, subject
to opinion.

Just as there are many souls
there are many Truths.

Everyone holds

to his or her own Truths.

However, through
the looking glass
of the actual
Truth is defined by
the veritable doctrine
of the landscape
and speaks from
the ground
of the beyond.

Then, the artist
pulled out of trance
feeling the higher order
of principalities.

It was that the other
side of being in time
constituted a one
dimensional existence
and the indwelling of
a vertical column of time.

As shadows of infamy
cast the ugly face of
being in nothingness
the artist painted
the savage likeness
of dread and despair.

It was the portrait
of pain screaming
in the last breath
of what matters.

It was the dirge
of drudgery occupying
space in time as the artist
drew a long look into
the madness of the world.

How pure music soothes
the heart in angst.

Then, the artist painted
the veritable Truth
of The Unknown God
as beauty, Truth, and love.

So, there were three
faces of the same image.

*

There is an uncertainty
to the winds
driven from time past
that defines the moment
when space in time
seeps into the interstices
of mind.

There is a Truth
to time past
that brings silence
to caverns of thought
as a dense fog
covers what matters.

There is a longing
for what matters

as the bones
of Truth crumble
before the living
moment.

Holding tightly
to pure music
mind trumpets
being in time
into the inevitable
as endless possibility
opens the heart
to the way, the Truth
and the life.

Seeing into a parabola
of time, the old man
reaches the substance
of being toward Truth
and time past passes
thought into forevermore.

It is that what
matters leaves
a trace in what
is there, as the heart
yearns for Truth
while being there
conceals life in
meaninglessness.

How the old man
looks through
a looking glass
to his place
in being in time

as volumes
of lost souls bury
the living moment.

Then, he feels the deep
touch of The Spirit of Truth.

Then, he awakens
to the way, the Truth
and the life, while
sitting beneath a white
oak tree.

*

CHAPTER 7: with The Spirit of Truth

Then, The Spirit
of Truth filled
the moment with life
and the will to be bowed
before The Unknown God.

Although being there
triggered itself
into the here and now
the will to be sought
freedom from twisted
rhetoric and the presence
of double speak disappeared.

How the longing
for beauty, Truth
and love weighed
heavily upon the mind
as thoughts pyramided
Lady Liberty into being
in time.

It is that being
in time fostered
life, liberty, and
the pursuit
of happiness
and the way
the Truth. and the life
became the doctrine
of the landscape.

As space in time
triggered the need
for faith, peppermint
birdie opened a nation
to being toward Truth
and peace beyond
understanding washed
across the earth.

So, the mysteries
of life marched
into awareness
for the children
of God, as the drums
of eternity defined purpose
in what matters.

It was the language
of beauty, Truth
and love that carried
now points into eternity.

Then, peppermint birdie
became the voice
of freedom across
the world, and she
was given the name
Lady Liberty.

While the purpose
of being there is
the pursuit of destruction
the purpose of being toward
Truth is to pursue life
onto forevermore.

Facing being in nothingness
the artist drew a figure
in the quagmire
of the madness of the world
and time edged him
ever closer to the ravages
of the war of principalities.

*

Facing being in nothingness
the artist drew a figure
in the quagmire
of the madness in the world
and time edged him
ever closer to the ravages
of the war of principalities.

As the destruction
of life, liberty
and the pursuit
of happiness dissolved
the figure into oblivion, time
pounded life into death.

It was a season
when chaos punctuated
the times with despair
and darkness filled
his heart.

He felt hopeless
in his helplessness.

Then, he worked
the figure into

a sunrise
where a day began
with the glory
of The Unknown God.

There was the pouring
of pure music
from the horizon
a rhapsody of beauty
Truth, and Love.

Then, he looked
to his muse
the scarlet rose
and time shifted
to the way, the Truth
and the life.

Then breath
returned
to the figure
and life carried
on to the earth
of what matters.

Then, the scarlet rose
sang the anthem of hope
and the artist
left his brooding.

Although jaws
of rage held him
his will to be
won the battle
of outliving himself.

He was free to live his life.

*

In the background
of space in time
where the will to be
dwells within life
liberty and the pursuit
of happiness Lady
Liberty takes her stand
against twisted rhetoric.

To deny the presence
of Truth is to give
into evil.

As a river
of thought streams
across horizons
of mind, the way
the Truth
and the life
pour pure music
into the heart
of being in time.

Then, the world
witnesses the presence
of The Unknown God
and humanity is
resurrected from
the grave of depravity.

It is the flood
of double speak

that drowns hopes
and dreams
as being there
corrupts hearts
and minds.

Pulling from beyond
Lady Liberty trumpets
the freedom of the will
to be and she announces
the Spirit of Truth
as a gift to the ages.

Then, the will
of humanity prospers.

Then, beauty, Truth
and love reign in space
and time.

It is being delivered
to the peace beyond
understanding that
awakens the desire
for freedom
as Lady Liberty charges
across horizons of time.

Then, the children
of God dance in the halls
of beauty, Truth, and love.

*

As the moon eclipses
the sun, space in time

spins in endless possibility
and this day sings beauty
into the here and now.

Where there is light
the vertical column
of time brings life
while the darkness
of despair leaves the drift
of things in themselves.

It is the beast
of being in nothingness
that hungers for life
while The Unknown God
gives the breath of life
to the living moment.

To see what matters
when out living self
dominates the will to be
heart takes to the way
the Truth, and the life.

Living beyond
the here and now
the will to be pyramids
the desolation of self
into the dust of mind.

Then, the old man
awakens from his
meditation, and his
life opens beauty, Truth
and love from the looking
glass of forevermore.

His inner eye follows
The Spirit of Truth
to the everlasting
as his faith takes his
soul to a house
of many mansions.

Feeling the peace
beyond understanding
he rides the rhythm
of the universe
onto forevermore.

Then, the pure music
of what matters triumphs
over the pain of being there.

Then, Olivia from oblivion
surfaces in the wind
and she dances across
the actual.

So, the moon showers
pure music into the heart
and space in time rejoices.

*

Crossing the bridge
of the here and now
to the beyond until
the fullness of time
called upon his heart
the old man turned
to the war of principalities
with power and strength.

The muscle of his
words broke the chains
of twisted rhetoric
with beauty, Truth
and love.

Then, he joined
Lady Liberty in
the battle for life
liberty and the pursuit
of happiness.

As his will to be
free toppled
the despots
trumpets of joy
and wonder infused
what matters across
the world.

It was the way
the Truth, and the life
that delivered humanity
to the epiphany
to the free and the brave.

It was the pure music
from forevermore
that opened his inner
eye to the glory
of The Unknown God.

As The Spirit of Truth
indwelled his soul
double speak disappeared.

As the old man
witnessed the actual
in the here and now
Olivia from oblivion
entered his life giving
him true love.

Registering in his heart
was the anthem of hope
as he framed the moment
with a parabola of time.

Then, the moon
eclipsed the sun
signaling the beginning
of the peace beyond
understanding.

*

As the drums
of eternity took
the living moment
into the unknown
a parabola of time
shifted the will
to be from
the here and now
and the scarlet rose
sang pure music.

Leaving what was there
the artist formed
the substance
of being in time, as blood
flowed from the moon.

Seeking the mystery
of life in hidden
meaning, they drove
on the rhythm
of the universe
to the other side
of being in nothingness.

It was a vision
of what matters
carved in the bones
of the skull, as mind
toured the unknown.

With the anthem
of hope saturating
thoughts with the mission
to witness The Unknown God
they steered themselves
to the way, the Truth
and the life.

How their purpose
formed the advent
of being toward Truth
as they listened
to The Spirit of Truth.

Then, they launched
into true love.

Then, they read
hidden meaning
as it flowed
with stardust.

It was a celebration
of faith that resounded
across horizons of time
as they married Truth.

Then, the drums
of eternity resounded
with the always
already there, bringing
the peace beyond
understanding.

*

Delivered from the jaws
of death, Eagle Hawk
crossed the unknown
with The Spirit of Truth
as his constant companion.

In Vietnam, where
the no longer waited
in the next step
he carried his faith
close to his heart.

With each breath
taking him closer
to being in nothingness
he looked to the way
the Truth, and the life
for peace.

His own life did not
belong to him.

Filled with the love
for The Unknown God
Eagle Hawk looked
to the light
of the vertical column
of time for his purpose.

It was the pure
music from one
dimensional existence
that brought him back
from an unmarked grave.

As time passed
into endless possibility
and wounded by
the war of principalities
he knew his purpose
as service to The Unknown
God, his destiny.

He carried a deep
smile with the presence
of the deep touch.

He knew the despair
of being in nothingness
when facing the certainty
of his own destruction.

He knew the pain
of seeing bodies
blown to bits
and the cries
of the wounded.

Years later
as a bar tender
he maintained his dignity
by being a good father
to three children
and a good husband
to Annabel Lee.

*

Dancing in stardust
surrounjded with pure
music, Annabel Lee
triggered the play
of a parabola of time
and the moment defined
the will to be.

How a tempest
of passion drove
her into epiphany
as she listened
to the anthem
of hope.

Unveiling the mysteries
of life with her fluid
motion, she followed
the way, the Truth
and the life onto eternity.

Then, the darkness
shed its skin.

Then, the light
of a vertical

column of time
broke through
what was there.

As space in time
flew into endless
possibility, Eagle Hawk
watched he undress
the moment.

It was a declaration
of beauty, Truth
and love that
carried his heart
to distant horizons
where he felt
life, liberty
and the pursuit
of happiness.

As her dance
lifted his mind into
a tender embrace
of what matters
the earth spoke
through the living
moment, and Eagle
Hawk called upon
The Unknown God
to bless their bond.

So, true love filled
them with pure music
onto forevermore.

*

It was the celebration
of the union of two
worlds that brought
the dawn
of everlasting love.

As time spoke
the separation
of hope from life
Annabel Lee joined
the tribe of Eagle
Hawk and they
walked hand in
hand into the province
of the unknown.

Wedded in the garden
of The Hard Rock Café
where the dance
of endless possibility
echoed in the hearts
of the children of God
Eagle Hawk took
Annabel Lee as his wife.

As they rebelled
against the tyranny
of twisted rhetoric
they spoke Truth
to power with hearts
dedicated to the way
the Truth, and the life.

Although the madness
of the world raged
with one abomination

after another
their minds were
set to bring beauty
Truth, and love.

Opening the living
moment with the light
of one-dimensional
existence, The Unknown
God poured pure music
into times and a half.

As The Spirit of Truth
forged the union
of two worlds
the scarlet rose sang
the anthem of hope
and eternity swept
the moment
into everlasting.

Then, the drums
of eternity pounded
the rhythm
of the universe
into the march
to always and forever
and a parabola of time
framed love as eternal.

*

The pure music
from eternity
fills the heart
with life, and the portals

of forevermore open
to the peace beyond
understanding.

Time and times
and a half flow
into endless possibility
and the artist sprinkles
stardust into the wind.

Picking up the flag
of purpose drives
the mind into circles
around hidden meaning
as the artist carves
what matters into the soul
of the will to be.

Then, the artist paints
his faith into the sky.

Then, clouds form
and rain falls
Then, flowers blossom
in hearts of gold.

So, the mind is
like a painting
of what is there
incapable to image
the actual.

So, Truth is the actual
living in things in themselves.

As trumpets

pyramid life
into the everlasting
The Spirit of Truth
gives faith
to the blind-hearted
marching into life
with the vision
of what matters.

Although hopes
and dreams assemble
reason to continue
being there threatens
times and a half.

To live without
hopes and dreams
is to dwell in
an unmarked grave.

*

As time wore
his mind thin
the artist found
an absence
in his heart.

It was that his passion
for art had been
lost and he stumbled
through time present.

His hopes and dreams
for representing beauty
Truth and love

had lost vision
in his message.

Coloring ideas with shades
of nothingness exploded
in his mind and his thoughts
went limp.

The no longer was
griping the muscles
of his heart and mind
as he lost the definition
of his being.

Singing the anthem
of hope, the scarlet
rose awakened him to life
liberty and the pursuit
of happiness.

Then, the freedom
of his will to be
found an image
that revealed
mysteries of life.

As he saw himself
as the messenger
of what matters
he marched into battle
with being in nothingness.

Returning visions
of beauty, Truth
and love, she opened
his eyes to the way

the Truth, and the life.

Filled with The Spirit
of Truth, she took
him out of his
dread, and the artist
saw his service
to The Unknown God
as his passion.

*

Thinking through
the corridors
of eternity, the old
man summons his will
to be into being in time
and the always already
there crushes twisted
rhetoric with the deep
touch of The Unknown God.

As the rhythm
of the universe takes
the living moment
into epiphany, he
places what matters
into the heart
of being toward Truth
and life throttles
through the wilderness
of the unknown.

Then,
the mystery
of life opens

his inner eye to the way
the Truth, and the life.

Then, the old man
believes himself
into the beyond
to march in the battle
of the war of principalities.

As time is redeemed
through the love
of The Unknown God
the here and now
drifts across endless
possibility
and the old man
envisions beauty
Truth, and love.

There is the dominance
of the deep touch
that crumbles twisted
rhetoric and Olivia
from oblivion dances
into his presence.

As she places
the drums of eternity
into his mind
The Spirit of Truth
carries him into the land
of the free and the brave.

Then, life, liberty
and the pursuit
of happiness

becomes the doctrine
of the landscape
and the old man
returns to the here
in now with his
faith ever stronger.

*

Triumphant over twisted
rhetoric and double speak
the artist witnessed
his destiny with what matters
as times and a half
demolished the citadel
of demigods and tyrants.

As pure music
surrounded his art
the existential threat
of being in nothingness
disappeared and hope
became the foundation
of the here in now.

It is The Unknown God
that emanates
love onto forevermore
as his muse topples
kingdoms of bigotry.

So, there is no place for hatred.

Then, times of dread
end, and mysteries of life
orchestrate dreams

of joy and wonder.

Then, Lady Liberty
marches across
the globe, bringing
freedom for all nations.

While in the pit
of desolation
where suffering longs
for death, the artist
follows the way
the Truth, and the life
as what matters
defines the doctrine
of the landscape.

It is The Spirit
of Truth that mobilizes
the force of endless
possibility, and only
God almighty has
the power to redeem
time.

Then, humanity dances
in the streets
burying twisted rhetoric.

Connected to one
dimensional existence
the muse takes
the artist to a world
of life, liberty
and the pursuit
of happiness.

Then, the soul
of the world rejoices.

*

Waiting at the edge
of space in time
for the rush
building inside
with what matters
peppermint birdie
slipped into a vast
sea of thought
as she fought
the demons of being
in nothingness.

As she looked
into the looking
glass of forevermore
the here in now
hounded her mind
with twisted rhetoric.

As she fumbled
without a purpose
Canis Lupus came
into her life.

It was a moment
that triggered
hopes and dreams.

Although staggered
by double speak
she turned to the way

the Truth, and the life
for the peace
beyond understanding.

Then, she read
a message from
The Spirit of Truth
written in her heart.

It was that Canis
Lupis was a free
spirit, searching
for Truth in being
in time, and the here
in now.

Then, what was
there confounded
her with trepidation
dissolved in the wind
and her heart felt
the presence
of The Unknown God.

As she felt
freed from
the madness
of the world
peppermint birdie
resolved to make
a difference
accepting responsibility
for her destiny.

CHAPTER 8: upon a midnight dreary

With electric thunder
racing through his
veins, and lightning
shooting from his eyes
Canis Lupis spear
headed revolution
across the land
of the free and the brave.

It was for peace
and the end of the war
in Vietnam.

Puzzled, the old
man wondered
what freedom
meant to the youth
of the day.

He did not think
hate speech
was an answer.

As time past
issued the rise
of passion against
all war, the old
man wondered
what happened to
live and let live.

It was that hate
festered in the body
of ignorance
holding little
value to human life.

So, a cause
blind as it may
be, fed generation
after generation.

It was the lost
generation that
found the peace
beyond understanding
through the way
the Truth, and the life
through the presence
of Jesus Christ.

Meditating through
times and a half
the old man saw
himself through
the persona
of Canis Lupis.

They were one and the same.

How passion was
wasted on his youth.

How freedom is
worth fighting for.

*

With her inner eye
Lady Liberty perceives
things in themselves
as the actual
fills her with the way
the Truth, and the life.

As she searches
the unknown for Truth
her will to be
unearths what matters
opening her vision
to one-dimensional
existence.

It is that pure
music flows
into her substance
freeing her to life
liberty, and the pursuit
of happiness.

So, who was once
peppermint birdie
has become
a pillar of hope
to a country of the free
and the brave.

So, Canis Lupis
ventures across being
in nothingness onto
the beyond where his
inner eye perceives
the origin of Truth.

It is that Truth
dwells in the beyond
to be visited
by those empowered
by The Spirit of Truth.

It is through
meditation that
Canis Lupis seeks
the indwelling of Truth
as space in time
configures the want
for a vertical column
of time.

Then, the anthem
of hope fills him
with joy and wonder
as he resides
in the presence
of The Unknown God.

*

With his inner
eye focusing
upon the actual
the artist faced
the existential
threat of twisted
rhetoric, as he read
between the lines
of things in themselves.

It was his connection
to the way, the Truth

and the life that enabled
him to dwell
in the beyond
while meditating
upon The Spirit of Truth.

Venturing far into
the unknown, he
felt the deep touch
as pure music
defined being
toward Truth.

Then, the artist
mapped what matters
in colors of stardust
as an anthem
of hope filled him
with a hunger for Truth.

Facing beauty, Truth
and love in the image
of the scarlet rose
he breathed
the substance
of being in time
an epiphany.

Although the moment
spoke Truth to the world
the world listened not.

As the scarlet rose
danced to the rhythm
of the universe
the artist dispatched

a vision of things
in themselves.

Then, they joined
themselves to each
other with passion.

Then, space in time
trumpeted being
toward Truth, and
they rose into
heavenly bodies
the domain of
celestial dynasties
and principalities.

It was the calculus
of what matters
that liberated them
from the madness
of the world.

Then, time passed
into distant memory
as what matters
surfaced in her mind.

In the center
of being in time
where pure music
founds its birth
in the beyond
the scarlet rose
brought thought

to surface
with power
and strength.

It was the muscle
of being toward Truth
in her presence
that took the artist
into a face bearing Truth.

As she danced
through his mind
the actual revealed
the mystery of life
as the way, the Truth
and the life.

Then, time stopped
in the awakening
to Truth.

In the feel
that tugged
on his heart
displacing
time in space
the colors
of what matters
trumpeted over
the despair of
being in time.

It was the existential
threat of twisted
rhetoric that left
time present and

the light of one
dimensional existence
brought his life
ever closer to
The Unknown God.

Although times
and a half visited
him with despair
of being in nothingness
the scarlet rose sang
an anthem of hope
taking him to epiphany.

Then, he hooked
himself to the rhythm
of the universe
pounding life with
the drums of eternity.

*

Then, the light
known to the moon
slipped shadows
that concealed
times and a half
as want colored
the night with wonder.

It was his driving
passion for Truth
that unearthed
the moment
where what matters
pyramided the surfacing

of what matters.

As the artist
drew the breath
that opened the inner
eye to The Spirit
of Truth, time
danced across
visions of the way
the Truth, and the life.

As a witness
to things in
themselves
he painted life
liberty, and
the pursuit
of happiness.

Following the flight
of Truth in
the moment, he
sketched the mind
awakening to a dawn
filled with pure music.

Although the moon
became a distant
memory, a message
transcribed an artifact
placing it in the here in now.

Looking back across
the night sky
the artist reached
into a vision

immersed in wonder.

How he felt
the blood of Truth
racing across his mind.

It was a meaning
echoing in his skull.

It was the consummation
of passion throbbing
space in time.

*

Although the night covered
the jungle with darkness
mortar fire pounded
thoughts with stardust.

It was a time
when Vietnam bled
with the lives of the free
and the brave, but that
was long ago.

The wounds
from that war
never healed
for some.

To remember
those times
erupted with
pain, dark
and foreboding.

It was a time
when dread flourished
in hearts and minds.

How sleepless nights
echoed in bastions
of hell.

So, it is times
long after
that the trauma
of being there
could not be
forgotten.

How senseless
it seems to die
without a cause.

Back home again
Eagle Hawk listened
to pure music
for comfort
finding freedom
to live.

Regaining his place
among the free
and the brave, he
saw in the night
the same moon
that shown back then
as he trumpeted
life, liberty and
the pursuit of happiness.

How feeling the dance
of beauty, Truth
and love opened
the moment to hope.

*

Annabel Lee listened
to the wind speak
Truth to the will to be
as clouds opened
the twilight
to forevermore.

It was the dance
of being in time
that tipped the scales
in favor of hope.

Then, pure music reached
deep within her heart.

Then, she looked
to the way, the Truth
and the life for comfort.

Although shadows
brought mindlessness
creeping from the West
to East, she felt the passion
of living in one
dimensional existence.

Trumpeting the will
to be over being there
she leaped to the other

side of space in time
as she dangled in the pain
of being in the age.

As a vertical column
of time eclipsed being
in nothingness, she
rode the rhythm
of the universe
onto the beyond.

Then, the crystal
crow took her
into the looking
glass of what matters
as the actual blossomed
with colors, radiant.

It was that she
trusted things in
themselves
the veritable
the actual, as
the wind shifted
patterns of light
and the trees revealed
the authentic article
of being toward Truth.

How she loved Eagle Hawk.

How being with him
made passion possible.

Although at times
he would brood

she accepted his
will to be as
a man of devotion.

*

It was stardust
written into her dreams
as the moon undressed
the living moment
and the drums of eternity
echoed within her
nakedness.

As Truth rang her skull
with the chimes
of pure music, she
pyramided life into
her living moment
and drums rolled Truth
into her mindscape.

Waiting in the sky
celestial dynasties
announced what matters
to a world hungry
for life, liberty, and
the pursuit of happiness.

How Truth mustered
the strength into the will
to be to conquer
the depravity of
being there as double
speak disintegrated
in times and a half.

Then, pure music filled
the air with the anthem
of hope, as she danced
through a wilderness
of dreams.

Looking through a portal
in a parabola of time
she saw the message
from the encompassing
as it wrote beauty, Truth
and love in stardust.

Then, the artist
pictured the coming
of the way, the Truth
and the life, and his
purpose to serve
The Unknown God
became clear.

So, the scarlet rose
blossomed onto the edge
of being toward Truth.

So, she saw her purpose
as a child of God
to serve and protect
her faith.

Although times of being
in nothingness were
in her past, she grew
with life, liberty
and the pursuit
of happiness.

*

Wearing a mask to
hide inherent evil
twisted rhetoric deceived
the world with its
sweet sounding music.

It was a type
of lullaby murmuring
softly with darkness
in its heart, and the world
listened, mesmerized
by the double speak.

It was the artist
that saw the malicious
doctrine. and he painted
the devastation of Truth
with the hope that
the world would see
what truly matters.

As it worshipped
the will to power
with derision
the despots erased
life, liberty, and
the pursuit
of happiness
 from language,

So much of the world
lived in darkness.

So, the artist pictured
the light of one
dimensional existence
as the way, the Truth
and the life.

To engage in the war
of principalities, he
spread beauty, Truth
and love from pure
music, and sowed
seeds of hope.

As the anthem
of hope found the wind
to carry across the globe
the will to be awakened
the children of God
to the existential
threat of tyranny
in the here and now.

It was the determination
of speaking Truth
to power that freed
the slaves from being there.

Although twisted rhetoric
infiltrated hearts and minds
with poisonous darkness
the artist equipped
individuals with the light
from The Spirit of Truth.

*

As a song of beauty
Truth, and love surrounds
times and a half
Eagle Hawk gave the moment
a second look at what
was there.

With liquid thunder
racing through his
veins, he felt
the power of the always
already there charging
passion into his here
and now.

It was the life
of vertical column
of time that unloosed
mysteries of life.

It was the way
the Truth, and
the life that
delivered beauty
Truth, and love
to visions of eternity.

Although echoes of war
confounded the world
he found the peace
beyond understanding
in his life.

Sitting on the edge
where being in time
bled streams of thought

Eagle Hawk saw in Annabel
Lee the pure music
that gave wonder and joy
that silenced the rage of war.

Then, the crystal crow
took his mind
into the dance
of forevermore
as blasts from bombs
banged in his mind.

How he felt his faith
soar as The Spirit
of Truth offered him
the deep touch.

How Annabel Lee
gave him the hidden
meaning of love.

It was his destiny
to connect what
matters to
the elements
of his will to be.

So, his love for
The Unknown God
mirrored in his love
growing toward
Annabel Lee.

*

So, The Spirit of Truth
indwelled the old man
as he trusted in the way
the Truth, and the life
and Olivia from oblivion
caressed his moment
with loving kindness.

It was a time when
they pyramided into
vast horizons, finding
the peace beyond
understanding, while
they were drawn closer
to The Unknown God.

Meeting in the subtext
of hidden meaning
they unearthed times
and a half, as their
meditation guided them
through the unknown.

Although the world
of being in nothingness
haunted times with despair
they purged themselves
of dread.

So, they met
in a pathway
of joy and wonder
as they focused
upon being toward
Truth.

Although their past
had separated them
with eons of double speak
they connected through
the honesty of their hearts.

Reading the writing
on the gateway
to Truth, they suspended
space in time with their
wills to be.

So, they met
things in
themselves
while being in
the actual.

It was that they were
together in their here
and now.

So, Olivia's astro
projection had carried
across eons until they
began their journey to
beauty, Truth, and
love, to the peace beyond
understanding forevermore.

*

It was Memorial Day
that they gathered
to remember the fallen
patriots who died while

defending their country
while defending freedom.

Eagle Hawk and Annabel
Lee led the procession
to The Hard Rock Café
followed by the old
man and Olivia from
oblivion.

The artist and the scarlet
rose marched on
the moment with Canis
Lupis and peppermint birdie.

A crowd looked on
saluting the star
spangled banner.

It was sadness mixed
with joy, as they revered
those who gave the last
full measure.

It was a triumphant
declaration over
twisted rhetoric
the infamy of tyrants.

When the scarlet rose
sang the anthem of hope
tears filled their eyes.

After they dined
on bar-b-que ribs
pure music led them

to dance
following the rhythm
of the universe.

It was a wondrous
celebration of freedom.

After a long day
of celebration, they
returned to their homes
and to the quiet of peace.

However, the artist
drew lines, orchestrating
images of war and peace.

It was a portal
in a parabola
of time, depicting
the blood lost for life
liberty, and the pursuit
of happiness.

*

Beneath the sun's broil
casting shadows of thought
the old man gathered wits
of being in time.

The brutal savagery
of twisted rhetoric
led his mind to
seek The Spirit
of Truth.

It was the depravity
in double speak that
captured a nation
although a remnant
of true believers
followed the way
the Truth, and the life.

A soul without faith
in The Unknown God
was lost in the chaos
of the world.

As the old man
plunged into meditation
through what was there
streams of pure music
encompassed the living
moment.

Riding the rhythm
of the universe
he found the breath
of enlightenment
as stardust lit the way.

Echoing in his mind
were things in themselves
and the substance of
the will to be.

How unearthing Truth
from the ruble
of being in nothingness
lit the way to life, liberty
and the pursuit

of happiness.

Attacking the body
of twisted rhetoric
the old man pyramided
the anthem of hope
as the new beginning
of the here and now
dwelling with beauty
Truth, and love.

Then, the old man
sat in the shade
of a white oak tree
with the deep touch.

*

To think upon the stars
in a night of pitch
how mind travels far
into the beyond
as her inner eye
fixes on a house
of many mansions.

There, on the other
side of being in
nothingness, hope
stirs the blood
of forevermore
as pure music
encompasses being
in time with beauty
Truth, and love.

Emerging into
the immediate
the vision of the always
already there speaks
to the heart
with power and might.

AQs time runs
with the rhythm
of the universe
a two-dimensional
existence presents a portal
to what matters.

Then, the artist
folds colors into
a maze of the actual
and hidden meaning
comes to view
through the inner eye.

Then, the crystal crow
speaks Truth to power
as twisted rhetoric
crumbles beneath
the crush
of the way, the Truth
and the life.

Although being in
nothingness echoes
across the here in now
the artist paints
The Spirit of Truth
unearthing the ground
of always and forever.

It is an orchestration
of what matters
in the presence
of The Unknown God.

How humble the artist
feels with his faith in
God almighty.

*

So, it was the warrior
blood in Eagle Hawk
that penetrated
the times and a half
of the world with
the certainty of
a bayonet to the heart.

As screams of the dying
broke a horizon of darkness
the wounds inflicted by war
surrounded the living moment.

To lie in a rice paddy
buried in the mud
while the stars were
beyond reach, he
learned the presence
of The Unknown God
in his life.

Then visions of Annabel
Lee fed his mind
with the will to be
to carry on through

adversity.

Although pain crippled
him for a time
Eagle Hawk climbed
into a moment
Eagle Hawk climbed
out of himself.

It was years later
that he found
the peace beyond
understanding through
the way, the Truth
and the life.

Taking his stand
in The Hard Rock
Café, he looked
to Annabel Lee
his treasure.

Although she was
busy, she looked
back to him
with a gracious
smile.

The artist was
there, sipping on
his Jack Daniels
sharing times
with thoughtful
fellowship.

Filled with The Spirit

of Truth, the scarlet
rose broke into song
and the anthem of hope
reached with the deep
touch, stirring hearts.

*

Caught in the rage
of war when blood
flooded the here
in now with dread
and courage
was his only option
Eagle Hawk holding his
ground as his wounds
broke the moment
with his will to fight.

Although years separated
the actuality of war
his scars reminded him
through dreams filled
with trembling.

How the pounding
of mortar fire had
crippled his life.

From the jungle
of immanent death
his will to be carried on.

Putting his life
back together, he
found being

a bartender at
The Hard Rock Café
helped him get
back his life.

It was there
that he met
Annabel Lee
a cocktail waitress.

He grew attached
to her with fond
affection, and
the regulars
at the bar bonded
with him as a buddy.

His favorites
were an old man
an artist, and
Canis Lupis
along with their
lady friends.

They became his
new soldiers in arms.

Together, they rode
the road to kingdom
come in the freedom
of the wind.

Gradually, memories
of the war, the dead
and the dying became
echoes, as he filled

his new life with freedom.

Because he was a survivor
he made the best of his life.

CHAPTER 9: to unearth hidden meaning

As the snow covers
the land with a blanket
of white, darkness
breaks into silence until
dreams of eternity dawns
in the heart of what
matters, and Lady
Liberty calls the children
of God to fight against
the madness of the world.

Drifting across horizons
blinding the eyes from Truth
the world has ripped
meaning from the words
of the deep touch.

Mimicking the call
to freedom, twisted
rhetoric confounds
nations with double
speak, and tyrants
slaughter the flesh
of the will to be.

As lives are lost
in the chaos of being
in nothingness, the blood
of Lady Liberty fills
the sea with despair.

Then, the wind carries

The Spirit of Truth
into the lives of those
oppressed by regimes
of darkness.

Then, freedom takes
to the streets, liberating
the here and now
from the grip of desolation.

Surfacing in minds
hidden meaning
holds across times
as Lady Liberty
reveals the drift
of beauty, Truth
and love living in
the mystery of life.

Bleeding across the sky
pure music reaches
into darkness
with the love
of The Unknown God
as the world hungers
for life, liberty
and the pursuit
of happiness.

So, the outcries
of the people
in darkness
are answered
with the experience
of being toward Truth
and the purpose of being

in time serving
The Unknown God.

*

As the moment
takes the old man
into a two-dimensional
existence, pure music
allows the will to be
to leap onto the other
side of being in nothingness.

As a parabola
of time focuses
the mind on a portal
to the beyond
faith conceives
itself into the way
the Truth, and the life
through the workings
of The Spirit of Truth.

So, the old man
transcends the madness
of the world
while Truth obliterates
twisted rhetoric.

Riding the rhythm
of the universe, he
reaches into epiphany
and an anthem of hope
defines the doctrine
of the landscape.

Then, true love
encompasses him
with kindness
and he feels
the deep touch
of beauty, Truth
and love.

Conquering the darkness
the light of one
dimensional existence
the veritable presence
of The Unknown God
allows the old man
to receive the love
of Olivia from oblivion
an extraterrestrial.

Although the age clogs
the times with doubt
she opens his heart
to what matters
bringing joy and wonder.

It is the triumph
of what matters
over outliving self
that fills the old
man with the promise
of endless possibility
including true love
and the peace
beyond understanding.

*

Probing onto the domain
of the light shining in a one
dimensional existence
mind travels
through endless
possibility to find
hope in the way
the Truth, and the life.

As she leaves the shadows
of being in nothingness
Olivia from oblivion uncovers
beauty, Truth, and love
that dwells in the presence
of The Unknown God.

Feeling the tenderness
of the deep touch
she breathes in
the passion
of being toward Truth
leaving the darkness
of being there.

Then, worlds and worlds
of tyranny collapse
as she reads freedom
into the bones of life.

Then, Olivia from oblivion
follows Lady Liberty
into the universe of life
liberty, and the pursuit
of happiness.

It meant victory

over twisted rhetoric
in the war
of principalities
as demons rushed down
a hill to drown
in a river of forevermore.

Encompassing the living
moment with pure music
she sees the splendor
of stardust
filling her mind
with visions of a house
of many mansions.

There are the drums
of eternity pounding
the rhythm of the universe
into her form
as her substance
flourishes with the anthem
of hope.

So, the power
of The Unknown God
dwells in a vertical
column of time
as the will to be lives
within linear time in space.

*

Fighting being in
nothingness in
the war of principalities
Eagle Hawk followed

the way, the Truth
and the life
to life, liberty, and
the pursuit of happiness.

Although riddled
with the sores
of despair, he gazed
into the looking glass
of the always already
there to find
the anthem of hope.

It was in his
meditation that
he listened to pure
music, stirring his
will to be.

Then, filled with
The Spirit of Truth
he climbed out
of himself with
his dignity intact
after reading
the writing across
the sky of stardust.

There was pure music
carrying him into
the substance of being
in time, as the living
moment exploded
into epiphany
and he became himself.

Believing in The Unknown
God, he found true love
as he surrounded
the demons
of the here and now
with his will to be.

Feeling the presence
of the way, the Truth
and the life, he knew
his soul dwelt
in a house of many
mansions, and the demons
that haunted the back
roads of his mind
fled into a herd
of pigs that drowned
in muddy waters.

Then, trumpets echoed
across the land
of the free and brave
announcing the advent
of beauty, Truth, and love.

*

From inside things
in themselves
the very substance
of what matters
and the beginning
of space in time
the old man launched
into the deep touch
the presence that

precedes understanding
and is the seed
of understanding.

While the old man
edged ever closer
to the mysteries
of life, those meanings
hidden from the known
and buried in the drift
of the unknown
he followed the footsteps
leading to the other side
of being in nothingness.

Then, the citidal
of twisted rhetoric
collapsed into ashes.

Whiled ideas were
juxtaposed, he
drew connection through
the pure music
of beauty, Truth, and love.

As the architecture
that formed
life, liberty
and the pursuit
of happiness
surfaced in the heart
of his will to be
trumpets opened
forevermore
and the drums
of eternity led

the march unto
the always already
there.

It was the beginning
of peace beyond
understanding
through the way
the Truth, and the life.

Gathering stones
of thought, he
built a house
founded upon
The Spirit of Truth.

Then, the old man
drew out of his
meditation, feeding
his will to be
with the mana
of being toward Truth.

*

As words release
the energy of thought
worlds collide
and the illusive
character of things
in themselves
connect meaning
to the muscle
of mind.

Delivering his soul

to a house of many
mansions, the way
the Truth and the life
forged a faith in true blood
and Canis Lupis wandered
through times and a half
to the root of meaning
giving life a direction
to the peace beyond
understanding.

Then pure music
eclipsed being there
with the true love
fostered by
The Unknown God.

Awakened by the sudden
shift to Truth, Canis Lupis
opened the mysteries
of life.

As the rising sun
of a new day
summoned him
to carry himself
into what was there
he saw the place
of concepts dance
in the air
and his will to be came
ever so much alive.

It was a matter
that led him
to the edge

where being in
nothingness dwelled
in shadows.

Attached to the rhythm
of the universe, he rode
waves of ideas
connected to words
as the sea
of what was there
filled him with life.

He was neither
there or not there
neither here or
not here, as
suspension held
him differing
and deferring.

*

Then, the wind blew
across the darkness
as silence fell
as the will to be
stood against the fury
of being there
that thrust a fist
into the face
of being in time.

It was the darkness
of twisted rhetoric
that corrupted
the language of being

toward Truth and
the children of God
as time withered the bones
of beauty, Truth
and love.

Breaking through the silence
piercing the darkness
with the light of one
dimensional existence
defending life, liberty
and the pursuit of happiness
The Unknown God
gathered the children
of God and they marched
against the citadel of hatred.

As pure music poured
from the heavens
the living and dead
raised their voices
praising the way
the Truth, and the life.

As a portal opened
in a two-dimensional
existence to the splendor
of a vertical column
of time, the drums of eternity
pounded life into the land
of the free and brave.

As the doctrine
of the landscape
wrote freedom
into the heart

of the world, Lady
Liberty opened
their spirits to
forevermore.

Then, the age
of fear ended.

Then, the children
of God danced
in the streets.

So, being toward Truth
was free to worship
The Unknown God.

*

There was among
bloodied briars
flowers that blossomed
with the scent
of eternity and the wind
carried that fragrance
across the universe
onto the living moment
of space in time.

As the rhapsody
issuing life, liberty
and the pursuit
of happiness toppled
the citadels pf twisted
rhetoric, the artist
chose to answer
the call of the way

the Truth, and the life.

Believing the awesome
power of The Unknown
God, he painted
the way through
the madness in the world
although he had been
thrown there naked
yet unafraid.

It was to face
the existential
threat he had
inherited.

Constructing a stance
against the forces
of double speak
he journeyed
into the darkness
of being there
following The Spirit
of Truth into victory
over the wilds
of the wasteland.

Through a two
dimensional existence
he portrayed the steps
to epiphany with the hope
in the connectivity
grounded in being
toward Truth.

As the images

of what matters
portrayed his
solitary odyssey
with a growing
want for beauty
Truth, and love
a portal to the other
side of being there
appeared, while he
rode the rhythm
of the universe
onto the everlasting.

*

As her inner eye
opened to the looking
glass of being in time
the scarlet rose
the artist's muse
his inspiration and comfort
how she brought epiphany
to his life.

Riding the rhythm
of the universe
she took the artist
through a parabola
of time to the other
side of being there
to the domain
of beauty, Truth
and love, the very
elements of eternity.

Filled with he Spirit

of Truth, they
orchestrated space
in time to the death
of twisted rhetoric
as the artist
composed eternity
from a grain of sand.

Then, their blood
carried stardust
into thoughts.

It was with the presence
of The Unknown God
in their lives that
they triumphed over
double speak
and the demons
in the here and now
vanished forevermore.

To be liberated
from the constraints
that bound them
in ashes, where
the wasteland smothered
the breath of freedom
the trumpets
of the always already there
announced the advent
of the light of one
dimensional existence.

Then, the scarlet
rose issued times
where the drums

of eternity pounded
life into his painting
grounded in the way
the Truth, and the life.

So, they brought
beauty, Truth
and love
from the beyond
to the here and now.

www.ingramcontent.com/pod-product-compliance
Lightning Source LLC
Chambersburg PA
CBHW071725120626
46550CB00002B/384